THE JOURNEY

Carolyn Corbett Tyndall

PRESS

The Journey
by Carolyn Corbett Tyndall

Printed in the United States of America

ISBN 978-1-60791-856-1

Unless otherwise indicated, Bible quotations are taken from the *New King James Version* of the Bible. Copyright © 1982 by Thomas Nelson, Inc. Used by permission. Scripture marked KJV is taken from the *King James Version* of the Bible.

www.xulonpress.com

DEDICATION

This book is dedicated to
Louie,
who is my fellow traveler
and one of God's miracles.

CONTENTS

PREFACE

All people, even Christians, have struggles and trials. The difference between those who are Christians facing difficult times and those who are not believers is in how they deal with their tribulations.

The trials Christians endure vary greatly. Some must suffer physical illnesses. Others experience the loss of loved ones. Some have to deal with broken relationships. Many parents have to cope with rebellious children. Add to these things struggles with financial problems. The list goes on and on.

None of us can know the tribulations we may encounter along life's journey nor how many we will experience. The certainty that we have, however, is that God is with His children every step of the way. He will always use each trial as an opportunity to teach His followers to lean on Him and to grow in our spiritual maturity as a result of His faithfulness.

This book is the story of one such trial that my husband and I experienced. It is only representative of the many tests that all of us may experience. The outcome may even be different for those who have had similar struggles, but we can rest assured that when we are surrendered to His will, all things will turn out for our good.

God has His own reasons for prompting me to share our story. However, I believe that at least one purpose is to share with others going through crises how faithful God is, how important prayer is, and how valuable and precious the support of loving family and friends can be to those enduring trying times.

Since ours was a medical crisis, I have chosen to change the names of all the doctors and other medical staff as well as other patients and family members I met along the way in order to preserve their privacy. I have, however, used actual names of family members and friends who played such a significant role in our journey.

Over all, our experience with medical staff was very positive. No comment about the care we received is intended to reflect poorly on those who ministered to us. It is the intent of this book to show concerns that family members sometimes experience when loved ones are in crisis, not to cast any blame on the source of the concern.

My prayer is that those who read our story will find encouragement in dealing with difficult times in their own lives. God is good. He is faithful. His love and provision are immeasurable. His grace is sufficient. His joy is unspeakable. His peace is everlasting. He meets every need.

Trust in God!

Carolyn Corbett Tyndall

PART 1

THE FIRST LEG OF THE JOURNEY

Chapter 1

Crisis

Be anxious for nothing, but in everything by prayer and supplication, with thanksgiving, let your requests be made known to God; and the peace of God, which surpasses all understanding, will guard your hearts and minds through Christ Jesus. (Philippians 4:6-7)

On March 17, 2008, my husband Louie entered Pitt County Memorial Hospital in Greenville, North Carolina, to have surgery to repair five abdominal hernias. The surgery was to be a routine repair performed laparoscopically, a procedure much less invasive than some of the other surgeries he'd had over the years. He had been on the blood thinner Coumadin for the preceding two months to dissolve a small blood clot in his leg, but his surgeon, Dr. Pendleton, had him stop taking the blood thinner a few days before entering the hospital. Once Louie entered the hospital, Dr. Pendleton placed him on a Heparin drip, another blood thinner, for three days prior to his surgery; the Heparin would be turned off during the surgery and resumed after the surgery to prevent blood clots.

Louie had the surgery on Thursday, March 20, and Dr. Pendleton said all went well. The surgeon said he had to push through a lot of scar tissue from previous surgeries and that he had placed mesh over Louie's entire abdominal cavity, even into the rib cage area. We had been warned that this surgery would have an extremely painful recovery period, but in a few weeks the pain was expected to subside. Louie had to spend the first night in Recovery because there were no rooms available by the time his surgery was completed, which was around 6 p.m. I was not able to see him until 9 p.m. and then only for about fifteen minutes. Since he was not going to be placed in a room, I spent the night sleeping in a recliner in the waiting room, visiting him every two hours for fifteen minutes each time.

He was very sedated, but when he opened his eyes, his only request was for something to drink or some ice chips. The doctor would not allow him to have anything to drink because it might cause nausea and lead to vomiting, so all we could do was moisten his mouth with swabs.

Louie was placed in a room in Intermediate Care the next day. Each nurse in Intermediate Care has only four patients clustered in a pod on the floor, allowing plenty of time with each patient.

For the next two days, Louie seemed to be doing quite well. I stayed with him Friday night, sleeping in a recliner in his room. He was able to talk to a few visitors on Friday and Saturday. Since he appeared alert and was doing so well, about 8 p.m. on Saturday I asked him if it would be okay if I went home for the night. We live in the nearby town of Ayden, which is only about ten miles away from the hospital. Sunday was Easter, and I thought I might stop by our church in Winterville, which is on the way to the hospital, for our short sunrise service before going back to the hospital. Louie seemed fine with this plan since he was still in Intermediate Care and receiving plenty of attention from his nurses.

I had been home only about two hours that evening when I received a call from his nurse saying that Louie was experiencing confusion and disorientation and wanted me to come back to the hospital. I was on my way in moments and back with him in 15-20 minutes after the call. His blood pressure was very low—about half of his normal pressure—and he was very confused. He said he felt as if he were going crazy. He asked me where the doors in his room led, and I told him one led to the bathroom and the other led to the hallway where his nurse's station was located just outside the door. I was very concerned because I had never seen him this way before on any of his many visits to the hospital, but I tried to reassure him that he was probably feeling this way because of his pain medication.

The nurses were very attentive and were, I assumed, in touch with the doctor on duty as they tried different things to get the blood pressure up. About 2 a.m. they told me they were taking him for a CT scan, which they did. He was brought back to the room about 3 a.m. Just moments after he was brought back to his room and the nurse had left, Louie said he was very hot. So I got a cool, damp cloth and put on his forehead. Then he said to me, "I'm going out!"

I said, "No, you're not!"

He said, "Yes, I am!" With that, he went into a frightening blank stare, and my heart sank. I just knew that he was gone.

Since I was already standing, I quickly stepped outside the door, but his nurse was apparently with another patient. I motioned down the hall for another nurse, and in moments there were several people working on Louie. Perhaps one of his monitors had alerted everyone of a crisis. I heard one nurse say that she couldn't find a pulse, and they were manually pumping air into his lungs.

I tried to stay out of everyone's way, but I remember one of the nurses telling me that I did not have to leave. As I watched from the doorway what was happening, I grabbed my cell phone and immediately called my daughter, Dana, awakening her from a deep sleep. She lives only minutes away—right beside us, as a matter of fact. I told her to ask our friend Cathy Cahoon to come to stay with her 3-year-old son, Jansen, and to come at once to the hospital. Although I didn't tell her, I really did not think at that moment that she would see her dad alive again.

The doctor was now standing at the computer just outside Louie's door and checking the CT scan. I heard him say, "There's blood in his abdomen," and with that, Louie was rushed down the hall to the Intensive Care Unit.

Thus began the journey.

As hectic as everything was at the moment, I asked if Louie's things would be all right in his room. I was directed to clear out his room, so I quickly threw all his stuff in his suitcase and plastic bags provided by the hospital and relocated myself in the hallway between the Intermediate Unit and the ICU unit. I called our son, Eric, who was hundreds of miles away in Minnesota, to tell him he needed to pray for his dad and that things were very critical. I also called my pastor, Grant Carter, to request prayer and one of our dearest friends, Bud McLawhon, who was also a deacon in our church. Dana and Grant and Bud all arrived in a very short time to wait with me in that lonely hallway just outside the ICU waiting room.

While I was waiting alone before they arrived, however, I began to pray in earnest. Though tears felt very near the surface, I felt that I absolutely could not fall apart at this moment. There were things that had to be taken care of, and I could not function if I fell apart. I knew the situation with Louie was very serious. I expected every moment that the doctors would be walking through that door to tell me that he was dead. Although I was already praying as I was making calls, I now had to have a very serious conversation with my Lord.

My natural instinct was to beg for mercy and healing for my husband, but I had been a Christian a long time and had finally learned that I needed to ask God for His will—His very best—whether it was my desire or not. So I prayed something like this: "Lord, you know my 'druthers.' I know you are able to heal Louie and restore him to health, and that is what I want, his family wants, and his friends will want when they learn about this. I don't know exactly what has happened to him. I don't know if he has brain damage and might end up totally incapacitated with no quality of life if he survives or what his state will be even if he makes it. So, Lord, I'm going to surrender him to You. I want what You know is the best in this situation, no matter what it is. If this is the time that you are calling him home, I'll trust You to help me cope with that awful loss. I can't deal with the magnitude of this crisis alone, so I'm trusting in Your wisdom to do what is going to be the best for everyone. With Your help, I can get through anything." It was very hard to say that prayer and mean it, but I had learned long ago that God was not going to listen to my mouth but to my heart. He knew for sure whether my prayer was sincere or not, and I had totally surrendered this situation to Him.

My mind raced through countless possibilities as I sat alone and waited, but a peace had quickly settled in my heart, and I knew God was in control. There was nothing I could do but sit and trust Him to do whatever He knew was best. I also made a commitment to God at that time that I would do whatever was required to stay with Louie if he survived and to care for him through this ordeal no matter how long it took.

Soon, Dana, Pastor Grant, and Bud arrived to wait with me for the news. I really don't know how long we waited. It seemed like an eternity before a nurse finally showed up and said, "I know the doctor will be out shortly to talk to you, but I can't let you wait in suspense any longer. Your husband is stable at the moment. You'll be able to see him soon."

Shortly after that, the doctor on duty that evening came out and talked to us. He thought Louie had had a heart attack, but somehow I knew that he had not; and his surgeon, Dr. Pendleton, who showed up shortly after, also did not believe he had a heart attack. This proved to be a correct assessment in the days to come. He had gone into shock because of the blood loss. They were transfusing him with whole blood to stop the bleeding. Surgery to locate the source of the bleeding and to make repairs was out of the question, as he could not endure another operation. The four of us were all allowed to see him briefly.

Only those who have been through a similar experience can imagine the scene in that ICU cubicle. I've never seen so many tubes hooked up to one individual. There were lines everywhere and a whole bank of monitors checking all kinds of vital functions. I wondered how the doctors and nurses could possibly monitor so many things at once.

Louie was on a ventilator and was sedated. There were lines going directly into arteries in both arms, a central line for meds in his chest, a line going to his heart, IVs—too many lines to count. But he was alive! God had brought him through the first few hours of crisis. However, God had not yet told me what His plan was for the final outcome.

Since it was Easter Sunday morning, Pastor Grant needed to leave to prepare for the sunrise service, which by now was only a short time away. Bud also had to leave, and soon Dana also had to go home to check on her son. She is a single mom, and she needed to be home when Jansen awakened in the care of Cathy so that he would not be upset when he realized his mom was not there. I knew that once she got him settled with another friend, she would return to the hospital to wait with me.

Much of the rest of the morning is a blur. I, of course, remained at the hospital. As the day progressed, friends who had heard the news at church began to show up, and I know there were people with me all afternoon and evening. There were countless phone calls, and our son Eric called at least five times from Minnesota to hear what was going on. I could only see Louie fifteen minutes every two hours, and all I could do was look at him and pat his hand or touch his face. It was hard to find a spot that was not occupied by some device.

In spite of the seriousness of the situation, I experienced such a peace from God. I felt God surrounding me and supporting me in such an awesome way that I was amazed at the peace I felt in spite of my great concern.

All day concerned friends prayed with me and comforted me as I recounted the story of what had happened to Louie. Words are so inadequate to describe how much I appreciated their support.

At the final visitation at 8:30 Sunday evening, Louie appeared to be stable. He was still receiving transfusions, but his heart rate and blood pressure looked good. I decided to go home. I knew that many patients' families opted to stay all night and sleep in the waiting room. I had done that myself when Louie had been in the hospital on other occasions. However, I hadn't slept in two days, I hadn't eaten all day Sunday, and I hadn't had a shower all day. I thought about staying, but I decided there was absolutely nothing I could do in the waiting room. Besides, they would not let me see him again until morning. If I were needed, the hospital would call me, and I could be back at the hospital in a few minutes. I decided that I would have to do the best I could to keep up my strength and energy because I realized this was going to be a taxing experience, so I came home.

I have never liked to stay alone at night. Even though we live in a very quiet neighborhood, the fact that we had been burglarized once while we were out of the house and on another occasion two masked men had accosted Louie outside, forced him into the house, and attempted to rob him at gunpoint contributed to my fears of being alone overnight. In addition to that, in recent years I had great difficulty sleeping soundly through the night under the best of circumstances. In view of all that was going on at the time, I antici-pated that once I got home, I would not sleep at all, but at least I could get a shower.

To add to the drama, when I arrived home and was preparing for bed, I realized that a diamond ring I always wore was missing. My first thought was that I had lost it at the hospital where I had washed my hands so frequently when entering and leaving Louie's room in ICU. I wasn't all that concerned about the monetary value of the ring, but the small diamonds in the ring were from my mother's and my sister's engagement rings. I had kept my deceased mother's rings for over thirty-five years and my deceased sister's rings for nearly ten years. It had only been a year since I decided to have the diamonds reset in a ring I could wear. I treasured it because each time I looked at the ring, I thought of my mother and my sister.

Now it was missing. I said to the Lord, "I'm so tired, Lord. It has been a very stressful day, and now to add to that crisis, I'm missing a ring that I'm very sentimental about."

I called the hospital to report the lost ring in case someone found it, but I suspected it was in a trash can along with a multitude of paper towels and would never be found.

As I talked to the Lord about the ring, I told Him that I realized what a small thing it was in comparison to the crisis I was in at the moment, but if He saw fit and it was His will, could He please restore the ring to me. I was too tired to worry about it, and I really needed to try to get some sleep.

Just before going to bed, I felt a need to check Louie's suitcase, which was still in the trunk of my car, to retrieve his cell phone so that I could charge it. As tired as I was, I plodded out to the garage, opened the trunk, scrambled through the suitcase, and there among his clothes lay my diamond ring. I could hardly believe my eyes!

I came back into the house, so joyful at finding the ring. Right away I began to thank God and praise Him that He had cared enough about something so insignificant in the big scheme of things as my little ring. It was then that God told me the most wonderful thing! He said, "Don't you know that if I care enough to take care of some-thing as small and insignificant as your little ring that I will take care of Louie in this big crisis?"

Such a flood of peace rushed into my heart with His words. I knew then in my heart that Louie was going to be okay. I believed that he would be restored to the health he had before this crisis, and that assurance came only from my Lord.

After I had praised and thanked the Lord for his mercy, I went to bed. I was asleep before my head hit the pillow. I slept like the proverbial log all night and did not move. This had to be supernatural sleep. I, who normally didn't sleep well and never slept well when I was home alone, slept solidly through the night—a deep, restful, restorative sleep. This was not to be the only night this occurred. In the days to come, I experienced night after night of sound, restful sleep. Each morning I would awaken refreshed and ready to face the new day. It would be one of the things that allowed me to have the strength I needed to do what had to be done. God is so good!

Chapter 2

The Travelers

My brethren, count it all joy when you fall into various trials, knowing that the testing of your faith produces patience. (James 1:2-3)

W ho was this man who was in such a crisis at this moment? He was my husband of nearly forty-five years. Louie was a young 73 years old. No one ever thought he looked his age. Only his white hair provided a telltale sign that he was now a senior citizen.

Louie had retired from the DuPont Company in Kinston, North Carolina, many years before. He had worked there as a manufacturing supervisor most of his career, following a stint in the Army and a couple of years of teaching after graduation from East Carolina College (University now). Having grown up on a tobacco farm, he always loved the outdoors and growing things. As soon as he retired, he not only spent time in his yard, which he dearly loved, but he also had more time to raise a vegetable garden. As a matter of fact, for several years he had raised strawberries on our small farm across from our home. At other times he had raised watermelons or pumpkins.

Louie is the outdoors person, and my hobbies are of a more sedentary nature, primarily reading and oil painting. Retirement for both of us has allowed us to spend more time doing those things we enjoy.

Because he was a workaholic and did a lot of physical work, he was always strong until the recent years when some of his health issues erupted. However, he continued to be very active, rising up after each medical problem to work hard again.

I had grown up in Ayden but had moved to Maryland to teach business education in the public high school there after graduation from East Carolina College. Although Louie and I were both in college at East Carolina at the same time (he was a senior when I was a freshman) and both were business majors, we never met nor remember ever having seen each other on campus. We did not meet until several years later.

After graduation, I taught in the public high school in Bel Air, Maryland, for five years before meeting Louie while visiting my family in Ayden. We became engaged after dating all summer while I was visiting my family. After we became engaged, I resigned my teaching job (on the first day of the new school year), taught September and October, moved back to North Carolina, and married Louie in November. We lived in Grifton the first two years we were married, and then we bought a house in Ayden, where we have been ever since. I thought I had left my hometown after college, and I never dreamed I would end up spending the rest of my life where I started.

After we were married I, too, worked a few years at DuPont as an administrative assistant until we adopted our first child, Dana. From then I became a stay-at-home mom, and three years later we adopted our son, Eric. I did not go back to work until they were 13 and 10, and then only on a part-time basis as an instructor at Pitt Community College. Working part time allowed me to get the children to school before I went to work, to be home when they returned from school, and to be with them all summer when they were out of school.

Later, while continuing to teach part time, I went back to East Carolina University and obtained a Master's Degree in education and became employed as a full-time instructor at PCC. When I retired two years ago, I was serving as department chair of Office Systems Technology in the Business Division. I always loved teaching, and I was especially blessed to be able to teach at Pitt Community.

Both Louie and I had professed Jesus as our Savior as teenagers. I have to confess that even though I attended church fairly regularly as a young person, I did not do much growing as a Christian. My church participation was very sporadic during college and my early single years as a working woman.

Once Louie and I were married, we both thought it would be important for us as a new family to be active in church, so we began attending church regularly. The Baptist church we joined in Grifton was right next door to our rented house—about 20 feet away, as a matter of fact. As we became involved in church, we took whatever church jobs we were asked to do. Both of us taught Sunday School classes, and over the years we took on other responsibilities as well.

When we had been married a couple of years, we purchased a home in Ayden. Once we relocated, we moved our membership to First Baptist Church in Ayden. We became active in that church and brought our children up to participate regularly in worship services and other activities there. Louie served many terms as a deacon.

About the age of forty, I became dissatisfied with my life as a Christian. Even though I was still teaching Sunday School every Sunday, I had some questions about my relationship with Christ. I was trying to be as good a Christian as I knew how to be. I tried to rear my children to love and serve the Lord, but there were issues about which I felt I had not found resolution. Things like loving our enemies or forgiving those who hurt us or our loved ones seemed biblical but unattainable to me. I knew what the Word said, but somehow in my heart I knew I did not have the kind of love for others that Christ had. I didn't really understand grace, and I wasn't sure about eternal security.

I went through a long period of seeking the Lord about these concerns. I heard a number of testimonies of people on a Christian television series that I thought were very excited about their relationship with Christ. Some of those people had endured devastating hardships, but I saw in them such a joy in the Lord! I wanted what they had, but I did not know how to get it.

I never told anyone about my personal search—not Louie nor my pastor nor friends. I just kept reading and studying and teaching the

Word and listening to others who seemed to "get it." I wanted all the love and joy and peace that I knew others had found. I kept asking God for it, and those I heard give their testimonies said everyone could have that same joy; but I had almost decided that I was an exception. Everyone else could get their peace and joy from God, but for me it seemed elusive.

Finally, after a long period of soul searching, I knelt one night in prayer in our small office while my family was asleep and surrendered my heart to Jesus. As I wept and cried out to Him, I gave Him everything I had! I told Him I would do whatever He wanted me to do and go wherever He told me to go. My words were something like this: "Lord, I'll do whatever you ask me to. If You want me to go to China, I'll go. If you want me to stand on the corner and hand out tracts, I'll do it. If you want me to stand on the rooftop and shout Your name, I'll do it." I wanted everything He had stored up for me. My heart was completely broken before Him.

Wonder of wonders, that is what He had been waiting for all along. He wanted my absolute surrender. Duh! Why did it take me so long to "get it" that I was expected to do things HIS way, not my way? I can't answer that except to say, thank God, I finally knew what it meant not only to believe with my head, but to believe with my heart in such a way that I trusted Him to be in charge of my life. He had become not only my Savior, but the Lord of my life.

Jesus answered and said to him, "Most assuredly, I say to you, unless one is born again, he cannot see the kingdom of God." (John 3:3)

That is when I was born again. I realize that the term "born again" has been ridiculed and abused in recent years, but that is exactly what happened. According to John 3:3, now one of my favorite verses, a man must be born again to have eternal life. I know for certain that my life really began at that moment. I walked about six feet off the floor for many weeks after that. I was on such a spiritual high that I never wanted to come down. God had given me a brand new spirit.

For the first time in my life I loved everybody and everything— even bugs, which I had previously detested. Now everything in life seemed to have a new meaning. All the creatures God had made seemed to have a new purpose. I wanted to embrace the world.

Suddenly, I developed a love for the Bible. I was not working outside the home at the time, but I could not get my housework done for the insatiable desire I had for the Word. I would read and read, finding scriptures I didn't remember ever having seen before and thinking how wonderful each new truth was. The Bible seemed so alive to me, and the scriptures were not nearly so hard to understand. I listened to Christian radio, and every sermon and song seemed meant for me. I was like a sponge soaking everything in. When guilt overcame me about some household chore I needed to do, I would put my study aside and try to accomplish my task. However, often I would have to return to my study again and again as questions arose in my mind that I had to find answers for.

Hymns and other Christian music took on a brand new meaning for me. I had sung many of these songs for years, but now suddenly the words had come to life. Often as we sang congregationally in church, tears would flood my face like a river.

For the first time I was realizing how much God loved me, what He had done for me on the cross, and how unworthy I was. Always in my life before I had wanted to do good but kept being discouraged because I kept missing the mark. Now I felt the presence of the Holy Spirit inside me giving me direction and the strength to do God's will. It was not that I ceased sinning, which I certainly did not and still have not done, but rather I had a new awareness of how my sins must hurt the heart of my Father when I disobeyed Him.

I now realized that I could never do anything well enough to earn my salvation. It was a free gift from God. Now my heart was so grateful to God for what He had given me freely, all I wanted to do was please Him in return—not to win His favor but because He had already given me His favor.

My life has never been the same since that moment. I have learned so many things since that time about my Lord and Savior, and yet I realize I've never even touched the tip of the iceberg that is God.

I would love to tell you that I lived happily ever after and never had another problem. That would not be accurate. Once I made a commitment to do things God's way, the tests promised all Christians began. There were to be many of them!

What can I tell you about trials? Not one of them has been a picnic by any stretch of the imagination. No, they have been hard and painful. However, never has my faith grown more than down in the valleys of trials. While I still enjoy occasional mountaintop experiences with the Lord and revel in the joy of those moments, it has been down in the valleys of life's hard times that I have learned of God's faithfulness.

He has never left me nor forsaken me, and I have absolutely no doubt that He will always be there for me. I reached a point several years ago that I figured God had already let me endure all the trials I needed to go through. Wrong! Now I realize that the tests get harder as we grow, and they are never going to be over until we go to be with Him in eternity.

I learned a lot about trials from my study of Job. While I've never experienced anything like what Job had to endure, I can relate to trials now as tests sent by the Enemy. I visualize Satan saying to my Lord, "Carolyn will let you down if you let me bring this particular thing upon her."

In response I hear my God saying to Satan, "Go ahead and test her. She will remain faithful to Me." What an awesome responsibility that puts upon me! When my Lord allows me to be tested, it is because He believes I will trust Him to get me through and remain faithful to Him. When I reflect on these things, I am reminded that God will go with me through every trial.

Is it fun to be tested? No way! Have I reached that point where James said we should "count it all joy" when we are tested? Unfortunately, I am not there yet. But I have at least come to the understanding that these trials will help me grow spiritually, and I can count it joy for the good that God will bring about as a result of the test. Is it an honor to know that God is trusting in me to stay faithful? You bet!

This is not said to frighten anyone who is considering surrendering to Jesus. The opposite is true. I'll take my trials any day with Jesus versus a life of comparative ease free of problems but without

Him. Experiencing His love and care and grace is the most awesome thing that can happen to any person.

I have realized all along that Louie and I are not the only ones being tested. I could share the stories of many of my friends who are also going through trying times. As I am writing this, one who comes to mind is a dear friend of mine whose husband has a debilitating illness and has recently spent several weeks in the hospital with pneumonia. He is currently receiving rehab in a nursing facility but is still unable to walk without assistance. My friend continues to teach every day and deal with some health problems of her own as she and her daughter, who lives with her, also spend time with her husband every day in the nursing home.

To add to all of the emotional stress of having a sick loved one, she shared in an e-mail this morning that her husband's Medicare ran out today. She is in a real financial bind to meet her husband's mounting medical expenses. On top of that, her daughter lost a jaw brace she wears to help with TMJ that cost $1500 while she was staying with her dad at the nursing home.

I sent the following e-mail message to my friend this morning in response to all her news:

> When it rains it pours! I'm so sorry to hear *[your daughter]* lost her brace. I know both of you must feel as if the world is tumbling in on you. When I hear all your problems or those of others, I am always reminded of something I *[recently wrote]* in my book. As Christians we are always being tested. While I've never compared myself to Job, I learned a lot by studying about all his trials. I try to picture some of his experiences whenever I'm being tested. I visualize Satan saying to God, "Sure Carolyn loves you and is doing your will, but I'll bet she will crumble if you let me test her with this!" Then I imagine God saying to Satan, "No she won't! Go right ahead and test her. She will remain faithful to me."
>
> That really puts a burden of responsibility on me to know that if God has allowed the test, He must believe that I have enough faith and trust in Him to get through it with His help!

While I don't welcome trials any more than anyone else, I am always aware that if I'm being tested, I must somehow be a threat to Satan! He wouldn't continue to plague me if I were not trying my best to serve the Lord. So, even though I don't relish these challenges, I do feel honored that God has allowed me to go through them—believing that I will stay faithful to Him and benefit in the long run as I learn to trust Him more each time!

Keep the faith, Baby! God is good, and He knows what he's doing when He allows these trials into our lives. We are going to come through these fiery tests like fine gold when they're over!

As always, you and *[your husband]* and your family are in my prayers!

Love ya!

Back to our journey.

Chapter 3

All Things Work for Good

And we know that all things work together for good to
those who love God, to those who are the called according
to His purpose. (Romans 8:28)

On Monday morning after Louie's crisis as I headed back to the hospital following that restful night of sleep, I felt surprisingly refreshed and was ready to hear some good news. I reflected on all the surgeries Louie had experienced in years past and how well he had done with each one. In 2004 he had been through a heart catherization and had two stents inserted in the blood vessel near his heart. Later, he had a cardioversion to shock his heart back into rhythm after experiencing atrial fibrillation.

In May of 2005 his heart went out of rhythm again, and he was hospitalized and put on an Amiodorone drip, which did bring his heart back into rhythm. Following that procedure, he had a complication with his leg, which was severely bruised as a result of the procedure to install a line in the groin to administer the Amiodorone. After a visit to the emergency room a few days after the procedure, he finally had to be admitted to the hospital a week later to check out the pain in the leg, which was by then quite black. The doctors did a CT scan to see what damage there was. I remember when Louie's heart specialist, Dr. Partele, came in and said, "There's good news and bad news. The good news is that there is no problem with the leg. The bad news is that the CT scan shows the tip of an aneurysm on the aorta."

I remember thinking and saying to Dr. Partele at the time, "No, that's all good news. If the leg problem had not required a CT scan, the aneurysm would not have been detected. I'm sure God has arranged this 'accident' to alert us to the need for attention to the aneurysm." I quoted my favorite verse, Romans 8:28, which says that "All things work together for good to them that love the Lord and are the called according to His purpose," and assured Louie and the doctor that this was still true. God had used the bad experience with Louie's leg to work for his good, causing the aneurysm to be found.

In early July a follow-up CT scan showed in more detail the huge aneurysm on his aorta—one of the largest the surgeon had ever seen. We had some anxious days awaiting the surgery, but the aneurysm surgery, called a Triple "A" procedure—short for abdominal aortic aneurysm—went very well. Louie had no complications, he had essentially no pain except for gas pains, and in a few weeks he was doing very well.

In 2006 Louie discovered an abdominal hernia. We were told that this is not uncommon for someone who has undergone major abdominal surgery. Louie underwent another corrective surgery to repair the hernia in June that year that required an overnight stay in the hospital.

In the months to come, Louie's energy level was very low, and Dr. Partele took Louie off the Amiodorone. His heart went out of rhythm again. In January 2007 he had to have another cardioversion. In March he needed yet another heart catherization. He was placed on a low dose of Amiodorone again to keep the heart in rhythm.

Later in 2007 Louie discovered he had five more abdominal hernias. In April he had another huge abdominal surgery to repair the hernias with mesh, and again, all went well. He recovered nicely. Once he was healed, he learned, however, that one of the hernias had been missed. He did not want to undergo another surgery right away.

In October of that year, doctors found another small aneurysm that needed to be repaired, this time with a stent applied to the artery instead of a larger, more invasive surgery. That procedure also went very well. However, in December Louie's family doctor found a blood clot in his leg that required another visit to the Emergency Room straight from the doctor's office. He had to be placed on the blood thinner, Coumadin. He had planned to have the hernias repaired in January of 2008, but that surgery was postponed because of the blood thinner he was on.

Later in 2008 when he finally decided to have the surgery to repair his hernia because it was getting so large, he learned through tests that the mesh had broken down on the previous surgery, and now all five hernias needed to be repaired. That is what had led us to this moment.

In all the other surgeries, Louie had not had complications—no excessive bleeding, no infections, little pain, etc., but this time He had not been so fortunate.

On my way to the hospital this Monday morning, I was optimistic that Louie was going to be okay. When I saw him, he looked good, considering all that was going on. He still had all the tubes, but I thought his color was good. He was still sedated and obviously not communicative, but he was holding on!

When I spoke to the ICU hospitalist, Dr. Gazelle, that day, she told me that she gave Louie a 50-50 chance to make it. As discouraging as that should have been, somehow I felt untouched by her news. I had already perceived that some of the doctors did not think his chances were very good. However, I shared with Dr. Gazelle outside Louie's room that Louie was a man with a strong will, a strong faith, and a ton of friends who were praying for him. Furthermore, I told her that it was not going to be over until God said it was over! She replied that doctors could use all the help they could get. She also admitted that he looked much better in person than he did on paper.

Transfusions continued during the day and into Tuesday. He was eventually given 5 units of whole blood, 4 units of plasma, and 2 units of platelets that I know of—perhaps more. It appeared that the transfusions were working and that the bleeding had stopped or at least slowed significantly.

Those long hours in the waiting room were made more tolerable by the visits of many friends and family members who came to sit with me. Their conversation and prayers were so comforting and helped keep my mind off the crisis at hand. I also began to meet others who were waiting those long hours for visits with their loved ones. Each weekday the hospital chaplain came to have group prayer in the hallway outside the waiting room for those who wanted to be a part of the circle. With all the prayers of the friends who were visiting us and those praying at home, the pastors who came and prayed, and the prayers of other patients' family members who could relate to our crisis, I felt completely bathed in prayer.

Sometimes I marveled at the peace I felt! I knew the circumstances of Louie's health were still very precarious, but I felt so at peace in the hands of my Lord that I did not feel the pain of uncertainty.

As mentioned before, one of my favorite verses in the Bible has always been Romans 8:28. I believe wholeheartedly that God uses ALL things to work for our good. I chose to trust Him from the very beginning of this ordeal knowing that whatever this crisis was all about, God was somehow going to use it for Louie's good, my good, my children's good—everyone's good. That's how He works!

Because of this truth, I began to look around me each day and think of what possible good was coming from each event. It's hard to describe, but I could feel God's presence as something like electricity in the air, and I knew God was busily "working things for our good." It was so fast and so consistent that I often felt like shouting for the very joy of knowing that He was doing His thing! Over the coming weeks, I would see more and more of what God was doing, while realizing that some of the "good" He was working might never be known to either of us.

In the first few days at the hospital, I had so many calls on my cell phone that Dana finally asked if I might have used up my minutes. I checked, and surely enough, they were nearly all gone. I decided to adopt Louie's phone for my own use. I also decided to personalize it to my taste, and I looked for the most positive song for my ring style that I could find. I did not intend to sit around with a long face looking sad and evoking everyone's sympathy. I could not see God's being glorified if my faith sagged or if I even gave the appearance of waning faith. This was the time to put my money where my mouth was.

Louie and I are now members of the Winterville Baptist Church and have been teaching alternately each month an adult Sunday School class made up of around 40 Christian men and women. If I taught dependence on God, I intended to live up to what I taught. There was no Christian song on the cell phone, but I chose "Singing in the Rain" as the happiest song in the menu. Each time the phone rang, I said to myself, "Lord, I'm in the middle of a storm, but I'm singing in the rain because You are in control. The storm is raging about me, but I'm in the eye of the hurricane and not touched by the winds at all because you have given me peace in the middle of the storm."

There was not a lot of laughter during this critical time, but one funny event does come to my mind. One day as I was sitting in the waiting room, I had several visitors with me. One of the visitors was my friend, Judy McLawhon. As we talked, I understood Judy to say, "Do you hear that saw?"

"No," I said, wondering why in the world someone would be sawing next door to the waiting room.

A few minutes passed, and Judy said, "Don't you all hear that song. It's 'Singing in the Rain,' and it's driving me crazy!"

"Oh, my goodness," I said. "That's my cell phone!" It had been ringing persistently in my purse as my daughter tried to reach me. I was so attuned to our conversation that I did not hear it. Apparently, everyone else in the waiting room except me had been hearing it. If I had understood that Judy was hearing a "song," not a "saw," I would have realized sooner what was going on. We laughed until we cried at that episode, and it was good to finally find something to laugh about. Judy told me to be sure to share that story with Louie when he was able to appreciate it. After that, I smiled every time I heard my phone ring with that tune.

A merry heart does good, like medicine, but a broken spirit
dries the bones. (Proverbs 17:22)

Each day of the coming weeks I purposed to be careful of my appearance. I tried to make sure my clothes were neat and that my hair and makeup were as presentable as possible. While I was eager each day to get to the hospital, I arose early enough to allow time to give this extra attention to my appearance. I did not want to look downcast. There is a scripture in Matthew 6 that mentions not letting anyone know when you are fasting:

> *Moreover, when you fast, do not be like the hypocrites, with a sad countenance. For they disfigure their faces that they may appear to men to be fasting. Assuredly, I say to you, they have their reward. But you, when you fast, anoint your head and wash your face, so that you do not appear to men to be fasting, but to your Father who is in the secret place; and your Father who sees in secret will reward you openly.*
> *(Matthew 6:16-18)*

Although I definitely was not fasting, somehow it just seemed very important in this situation for me not only to be strong in the Lord but to give the appearance to others of that trust I had in Him. I wanted my testimony of God's peace and grace to be evident. He was doing His part to keep me at peace, and I needed to do my part to be sure that peace was reflected in my countenance. I was not seeking the admiration of others; in my heart, I only wanted Christ to be glorified in me. Also, I wanted to look my best for Louie each day in case he opened his eyes. I did not want him to think I looked tired and bedraggled and worried, which would have made him realize how critical his own situation was.

There were many occasions when my friends and even Dana commented on my strength, probably because they did not see me crying or looking sad. I am by nature a very emotional person. However, often I do not cry when situations are very critical. I am much more likely to cry if I share some portion of my testimony or a faith experience or tell of something God has done for me or others. I just felt in this situation that if I ever started to cry, I would completely lose everything. I wasn't suppressing grief; I was trying to put all my cares on Jesus' shoulders. I was not being modest when I protested that this was not my strength but the Lord's. It was simply the truth. I told them that in my natural flesh I was merely a pile of mush. They needed to see that it was only God sustaining me moment by moment. I never, never wanted to take credit for anything He was doing!

Always in the past when Louie had been facing a surgery, I had requested prayer from our friends by sending e-mails to our contact list. I had already sent one prior to Louie's surgery this time requesting prayer and another right after the surgery assuring everyone that all went well. By Monday night, it was time for me to send a message to everyone telling them of the new turn of events and asking for their prayers again.

This became my pattern each night after coming home from the hospital. My e-mail lists (I had so many names that I actually had to make two contact groups) eventually grew to 67, most of them representing couples or whole families. Not only were all these people praying, but they began requesting prayer in the many churches of which they were a part. Many of these people have since shared with me that they forwarded my e-mails to their friends and family members. In addition to people on my list all over the United States and as far away as London, there were many others I didn't know in faraway places around the world who were praying.

Louie and I had been very active in Baptist Lay Renewals all over North Carolina for twenty years, and we had made many Christian friends in churches all over the state. These people were contacted by other team members, and they also were praying.

For those not familiar with a Lay Renewal, I'll explain. A Lay Renewal Weekend begins when the pastor of a particular church invites a team of lay people to come for the whole weekend to share with the home church. The team is never exactly the same on any two weekends, but the couples who coordinate the renewals choose from among all those who have agreed to help with such a weekend the ones they believe God leads them to invite to serve on a particular visiting team.

It usually takes several months to a year for a church to prepare for such a renewal. The visiting team is invited by the team coordinators and then officially by the home church. The weekend is generally preceded by a 24-hour prayer vigil by the home church. Visiting team members arrive on a Friday afternoon and gather for a team meeting with the pastor and the home church chairperson. After the meeting, the whole church participates in a dinner that may be a covered dish supper or a catered meal.

Following the meal, the church members and visiting team members assemble in the sanctuary for prayer and special music provided by the visiting team. Then there are special testimonies given by two or three team members who share what God has done in their lives and how He is using them. Team members are not told when they may be called upon for a testimony until the team meeting, so testimonies are essentially spontaneous and are given as led by the Spirit rather than from prepared speeches.

The congregation then divides into small groups that will each be led by one or two team members. There are no sermons nor teaching, only sharing in the small group environment. The focus of the discussion is for those present to search their hearts for a deeper understanding of their relationship with Jesus. Special team members also work with children and youth groups during this time.

The congregation comes back together for a joint sharing time in the sanctuary before being dismissed for the evening. Visiting team members are housed in the homes of the church members. Somehow God always places each team member in exactly the right host home. I've personally seen and heard of so many blessings coming from the times of sharing between individual team members and their hosts.

On Saturday morning, following another team meeting, team members are sent by pairs to church members' homes where a number of coffees have been scheduled to accommodate the entire adult congregation. After refreshments, another small sharing group time is held in the homes.

After the coffees, the team and congregation meet for lunch at the church. After the meal, the men all go into a group session, and the women go into their group. Another time of sharing and/or testimony led by visiting team members is experienced in a somewhat larger group.

When these groups have finished, there are a couple of hours of rest time for all those participating. In the evening, another assembly is held in the sanctuary after another meal for the entire church and guests. It is obvious we Baptists like to eat.

This time of testimony and prayer and special music is followed by another round of small groups. The evening closes with a final assembly in the sanctuary.

On Sunday mornings the team uses the Sunday School hour to lead the final round of small groups in Sunday School classes. They also use the worship hour for another time of music, prayer, and testimony. At the end of the service, an altar call is extended by the pastor to those who would like to make a deeper commitment to the Lord, to accept Christ, to move their membership, or to come to the altar for a time of prayer.

While these are the details of the format of Lay Renewals, one cannot describe all the spiritual growth that takes place during such a weekend. It is phenomenal! Having experienced a Lay Renewal in my own church before becoming a team member, I can attest to the change it made in my life and the lives of our membership. As a team member, I have also seen the response of hundreds of Christians in the many churches I've visited over the years as they are also touched by God and seek to make new commitments to Him.

The Lay Renewal does not end on Sunday. On the contrary, it is just the beginning of a new spiritual journey. Many church members sign up to participate in continuing small groups in the weeks following the Renewal Weekend. Most churches continue the renewal process by having a Lay Ministry Weekend the following year where the focus is on the use of spiritual gifts.

Just as no two teams are exactly alike, no two churches are exactly alike. Because what is happening during one of these weekends is supernatural and Spirit led, each church fellowship seems to find whatever it needs to make renewal in members' lives a reality.

Every visiting team member I have ever heard discuss Lay Renewal can tell that those on the team who go to serve end up with the biggest blessings of all. It is such a joy to be a part of what God is doing to draw His children closer to Himself. Participating in

Lay Renewals has led to my forming lasting friendships with many, many team members and countless individuals in churches where we have visited.

Besides the many people with whom I had become acquainted through Lay Renewals who were praying for us, in the coming weeks, I met strangers who learned of Louie's circumstances and offered to add him to their prayer lists and the prayer lists of their churches. It would be interesting to know how many hundreds, maybe thousands, of people interceded for Louie and me and our family in prayer.

> . . .*pray for one another, that you may be healed. The effective, fervent prayer of a righteous man avails much.*
> *(James 5:16)*

One incident I recall happened at a doctor's office. I had an appointment for a doctor's visit that had been scheduled before Louie's surgery. Since the appointment was set for 10 a.m., I called the doctor's office, which was located quite near the hospital, and requested an earlier appointment so as not to miss my visit with Louie in ICU at 10:30 that morning. They were kind enough to allow me to come in at 8 on the day of the appointment.

When I arrived, I thanked the receptionist for allowing me to change my appointment so that I would not miss my first visit of the day with my husband who was in ICU. Although I did not know this lady, she expressed concern about Louie's situation and said she would pray for him. I took a seat to wait for the doctor, and this lady called me back to the front desk. "What is your husband's name?" she asked. "I'd like to put him on my church's prayer list tonight." Of course I gave her that information and was grateful for her concern.

On another occasion I had to visit our bank to take care of a financial matter. I was in the office of one of the employees, whom I knew only on a professional level. She also had another employee with her that day whom she was training. I explained the financial matter I needed to take care of and that the reason I was doing so was because of my husband's crisis. I did not want to take a lot of their time since it was a business office, but I found them very interested in what had happened to Louie. They drew out much of his story with their questions and concerns and told me they, too, would be praying for him. They encouraged me to keep them posted on his progress. I was surprised, but pleased, to find busy people in the workplace who took time to show compassion and Christian concern.

In the waiting room at Pitt Memorial one day, I had a visit by the pastor of the First Pentecostal Holiness Church in Greenville, Rev. Paul Brafford. Although I had met him previously, I really did not know him personally. He was the pastor of a friend of ours, Dana Brown, who was also his secretary. She had mentioned Louie to him and asked for his prayers. He found me in that waiting room and had a time of prayer with me.

Besides my own pastor, Rev. Grant Carter, who faithfully came almost every day we were in Pitt Memorial, many other pastors stopped by to check on Louie and to have prayer with us. Rev. Bill Gay, who was our former interim pastor, came; Rev. Phil Frady, who is our associational missionary and a member of our church, visited; Rev. David Langley, pastor of Winterville Free Will Baptist Church, was there nearly every day to visit with me and others; Rev. Grover Everett, retired pastor and member of our church came; Rev. Frank Tripp, pastor of Church of God in Ayden and also Louie's barber, visited; Rev. David Welch, pastor of Spring Garden Baptist Church, Louie's childhood home church near New Bern and a church where we had helped with a Lay Renewal, came several times; Rev. Ronnie Hobgood, who is pastor of LaGrange Free Will Baptist Church and is also my cousin's husband, visited. I believe each of these pastors requested prayer of their congregations. Friends who visited told me the congregations of all the churches in Ayden were praying for Louie.

With all this prayer, who could help but feel the peace of God!

Chapter 4

The Power of Prayer

Peace I leave with you, My peace I give to you; not as the world gives do I give to you. Let not your heart be troubled, neither let it be afraid. (John 14:27)

I can do all things through Christ who strengthens me. (Philippians 4:13)

On Tuesday the doctors wanted me to sign for permission to insert a filter to prevent the existing blood clot in Louie's leg from moving to his lung. They could not continue to give him all the blood thinner due to the threat of further hemorrhaging, so the clot in his leg could present a problem if it happened to move.

I had never had to sign for any surgical procedure for Louie. The doctors had to share with me the risks involved in the procedure, and I had to make a rather quick decision as to what I would do. I said a quick prayer to God, and following the best advice of the doctors who should know what was best, I signed for the procedure. This would be the first of many procedures I would have to sign for.

This brought to my mind an event that happened shortly before Louie went into the hospital. We had both talked for years about our need to update our wills. They had not been updated since our children were quite young, and obviously there was no need now to specify how our children were to be taken care of since Dana and Eric were both grown.

A couple of weeks before Louie went in for surgery, I began to feel an urgency to take care of this legal matter. I told Louie I had made an appointment with our lawyer to update my will. If he wanted to take care of his, we could do it at the same time. He agreed that this was a good idea. Because a friend had recently mentioned the need for couples to have powers of attorney for each other, I decided to take care of this at the same time, and Louie decided to do likewise. I had no premonition that anything was going to happen to him, but my concern was what if something happened to me. We signed the new wills and powers of attorney a week before Louie went into the hospital.

As I thought of this in the hospital, I could not help but be grateful for the decision I had felt led to make regarding the powers of attorney. In the coming weeks, it made things so much easier as I began to handle financial matters for Louie as well as the many medical decisions I had to make. I saw this as yet another of God's blessings.

The good news for this day was that the procedure to insert the filter went well. Doctors also removed a line going into Louie's heart since tests now confirmed there had not been a heart attack. They also were able to remove a line going directly into the artery of his arm. They told me they were cutting down on the sedation and were hoping he would wake up soon. He was beginning to move his feet and arms as much as he could with the restraints.

I told the doctors and the nurses that Louie was experiencing his worst nightmare! His worst fear was of being pinned down, unable to move. He had seen a friend succumb to Lou Gehrig's Disease. It had broken his heart as he watched that young man, whose mind was still perfect, trapped inside a body that eventually was unable to move at all. Louie did not even like to have heavy covers on his feet while in bed because he felt the weight held him down. I knew that if he awoke and could not move, he would be extremely distressed. I was anxious for him to awaken, but I dreaded having him know that his arms were in restraints. I tried to be grateful for the fact that he was so sedated he did not have to experience the pain from the surgery he had been through nor was he aware of the restraints.

Some of the doctors were now more optimistic and were telling me that they expected Louie to make a full recovery. I had believed this all the time!

In the next couple of days Louie continued to make small improvements. His eyes would open slightly for just a moment, but there was no indication of any kind of recognition of me or others or anything else that was going on around him. Each time he would start to awaken, he would become agitated and his blood pressure would rise and his respiration would increase. Then the nurses would have to give him more sedation.

Doctors were anxious for Louie to wake up so that they could begin to wean him off the ventilator. They told me that if he were not weaned from the ventilator soon, they would have to do a tracheostomy. Also, the longer he was on the ventilator, the more likely he would be to develop pneumonia or another infection.

I was personally anxious for him to wake up for another reason as well. While I did not discuss it with family or friends, in my heart I was very concerned about the possibility of brain damage during the time Louie's body had been deprived of oxygen due to a diminished blood supply. I knew he had been experiencing disorientation and confusion for five hours before having been taken to ICU. I did not have the medical information to know how serious this threat was, but I was very troubled by the possibilities.

I requested prayer each day from my prayer partners online. By Friday doctors were able to remove Louie's ventilator, and he was breathing on his own. Unfortunately, after a day and half his breathing became too labored, which raised his blood pressure, and he was unable to cough up the secretions in his lungs. He had to be put back on the ventilator. This was one of the setbacks that doctors had warned me about, telling me that there were definitely going to be some ups and downs in Louie's progress. It was disappointing, of course, but I tried to rest in God's assurance that everything was going to be all right and trust Him to do it in His time, not mine.

Even though Louie didn't open his eyes, the family members and I felt that Louie was aware of our presence. I had been watching his monitors since he had been in the hospital. I had no medical training, but I asked a lot of questions. I already knew about his heart rate, heart rhythm, blood pressure, and oxygen level. I was beginning to learn about the stats on the ventilator as well. When I didn't understand what was going on, I asked the nurse on duty. I also tried to make sure that he was being turned regularly to prevent pressure sores.

He was becoming quite swollen from fluid that accumulated because of his inactivity, but doctors and nurses assured me that this was normal because of his inactivity. I later learned that he had put on more than 50 pounds of fluid. His arms and legs were huge, and his fingers looked like sausages. They attempted to prevent blood clots in his legs by using SCDs (sequential pressure devices). These plastic sleeves on his legs were pressurized by a compressor to help keep the blood flowing to his heart.

On Sunday, a week after the crisis began, doctors decided to begin feeding Louie through the tube in his nose instead of by IV. He continued to have a lot of lung secretions, so doctors ordered another X-ray. It didn't show any evidence of pneumonia, but doctors said sometimes it took a while for pneumonia to show in X-rays. At times his breathing rate would increase, and Louie would have to be given more meds to calm him down.

A few days after Louie began receiving food by tube, I learned from his nurse that he was also being given insulin. I asked why he was getting the insulin and was told he had diabetes. I quickly informed them that he did not have diabetes when he came into the hospital. They said that he must not have been aware that he had it. I assured them that he had been tested for diabetes by his family physician previously and definitely did not have diabetes. Then they told me he must have been borderline and that the trauma he had experienced pushed him over the line.

Apparently I wasn't going to win this argument. If his constant blood tests were showing he needed insulin, then so be it. However, I had heard of others who developed diabetes while in the hospital. I told his nurses that I certainly hoped this malady would go away when he was better. They did not give me very much hope that this would happen, but it was another thing I added to my prayer list.

Dr. Pendleton had mentioned to me at some point that if Louie did not wake up soon, he was going to order a CT scan of his brain. This added to my concern about possible brain damage and made me even more anxious for him to awaken. I felt that if he awakened totally, I would be able to determine if everything was all right with his mind.

By Tuesday, April 1, I was writing to my e-mail prayer partners that there was good news and bad news. Louie's breathing was much more normal, which was good; but now he had a staph infection and a stomach bug. His central line was changed from one side of the chest to the other in case it was the source of the infection, another procedure I had to sign for.

I was still not sure about the pneumonia, but doctors had started Louie on antibiotics for the infections. His blood pressure and heart rate were doing fine. He was once again very sedated, and doctors said he would likely not be waking up until the following week—not the news I wanted to hear.

This was another setback, but I was determined to focus on the reality that God had spared him thus far, and I believed he would still make a full recovery. Apparently, this was going to be a longer journey than I had originally thought from the beginning. I gave thanks again for the fact that Louie was not experiencing the terrible pain associated with his surgery as long as he was sedated.

The nurses attending to Louie appeared to be very attentive. The doctors seemed to know what they were doing. Occasionally I had to deal with a doctor's arrogance, but I felt I could overlook that as long as the doctor was competent and taking good care of my husband.

On Thursday, April 3, I sent the following e-mail to my friends, Sims Poindexter and her husband Bill, after she had encouraged me to keep the e-mails coming. I had feared that everyone on my list was getting tired of being inundated with "Louie Updates." Sims was also concerned about my well being.

Thanks, Sims. We love you both so much, and as always we really appreciate your prayers.

Please don't worry about me. I am walking in God's supernatural strength right now. I am tired at the end of the day, but not completely worn down. I try to get to bed as soon after 9:00 as possible, and except for a couple of nights, I have slept like a log. I know without a doubt that all the prayers being lifted for me, as well as those for Louie, are making all the difference. I feel as if I'm in a bubble of prayer. So many friends stop by each day, and they help to pass the time. Yesterday I had eight or nine people there at one time! They pray with me and encourage me and sometimes help me laugh! I think there have been 5 or 6 pastors, including my own, who have stopped by several times each and prayed and blessed me. Today some of the teachers I worked with at Pitt Community College are coming by the hospital to take me to lunch in the cafeteria. God has not forsaken me!

God is good, and while there are days when things aren't moving in the direction I would like, I have to continue to trust that everything is in His hands and that "all things are working for our good" in spite of the crisis. I continue to feel that He is working mightily in the midst of it all.

There are so many families in the waiting room each day who are going through crises with their loved ones. We have become a family who pray together, rejoice at the good news, and offer encouragement when things take a downward turn. Even if a few minutes pass when I don't have any visitors, I have the opportunity to share with this new "family."

I continue to pray that God will heal Louie and return him to perfect health, because those are my "druthers." I have my moments when I feel anxious, but ultimately I have to confess that He is God, and I am not! He is in control, and I can trust Him!

Have a blessed day. Love you much!

Louie had a tracheostomy on Thursday, April 3. I hated that it was necessary, but I realized he was probably more comfortable with the trach than with the ventilator tube in his mouth. By the next day, Dana thought her dad looked less stressed with the trach than he had with the ventilator tube in his mouth. At times he seemed more alert, but he was still unable to focus directly on anyone. His white blood count was down, his kidney function had improved a little, he did not have a fever, and his blood pressure and heart rate were good. We felt Louie was about to turn a corner in his progress. I was looking forward to seeing him removed from ICU and sent to Intermediate Care where I would be able to stay in the room with him day and night.

Part of my e-mail to by prayer partners on Saturday, April 5, described how I was feeling.

I want each of you to know that in the midst of this ordeal, I have felt the mighty presence of the Lord. His love—and your love—have surrounded me and brought me such peace and comfort and strength that it is hard to describe. Through this whole trial I have felt the assurance that all things are working for our good—even this. I'm not sure exactly what God is doing, but I can feel His positive actions all around me! Maybe one day we will know what God is up to, but whether we ever know or not, we can rest on Romans 8:28! God is good, and His faithfulness never fails!

God bless you!

Chapter 5

Amiodorone War

These things I have spoken to you, that in Me you may have
peace. In the world you will have tribulation; but be of
good cheer, I have overcome the world. (John 16:33)

I had never followed closely what medicines Louie took. I knew
about a few of them, but I did not know every medicine he was
taking. Besides that, his medicines frequently changed. I knew he
had been on blood thinner because that was a major concern before
his surgery. I knew he took medicine for his cholesterol and a couple
of others, but I did not have a complete mental list.

While sitting in the waiting room one day, it was a surprise to me
when the thought entered my head to ask the nurses if Louie were
still receiving his Amiodorone. I did know about this drug because
it had been given to Louie to control his atrial fibrillation.

When I went back to ICU for my next visit, I said to the nurse,
"He is still getting his Amiodorone, isn't he?"

"No," she said, "there is no record on the computer that he was
on Amiodorone."

"Well, he was," I said. "As a matter of fact, I saw the nurse give
him some when he was first admitted while he was awaiting surgery.
It should certainly be in the hospital's computer."

Someone from Pharmacy came to check on Louie's meds. She
looked again, but there was no record of his having been on that

drug. I was very concerned because he already had enough problems at this time without having his heart go out of rhythm again.

The pharmacist asked if I had a list of all his meds, which normally he took to the hospital with him. "No," I replied, "but I do have his bag of meds in the trunk of my car."

She requested that I bring them in for her to take a look. I retrieved the meds from the car, and there was the Amiodorone along with several others. She made a list of all his meds before surgery. Then a thought occurred to me that I shared with her.

"You know, I believe his heart doctor, Dr. Partele, had reduced the dosage on this medicine, and he was taking less than what is on the bottle. I believe he was taking half a pill (100 mg) once a day instead 200 mg twice a day."

I could not believe my own statement as I shared this information. Why in the world would I have remembered this? As I said before, I did not usually pay any attention to Louie's medicines. I could only believe that God had prompted me to check on this matter. If God had prompted me, it must be really important!

I made a phone call to Dr. Partele's office to confirm the reduced dosage, and the ICU nurse assured me that Louie would be placed back on Amiodorone.

This battle was not over. A few weeks later I felt led to ask again if Louie were still getting his Amiodorone. "Oh, no," the nurse said. "His heart rate and rhythm have been just fine. He doesn't need it."

"Wait a minute," I said. "You don't understand. He doesn't take it when his heart goes out of rhythm. He takes it all the time to keep his heart in rhythm." The nurse assured me he would check with the doctor.

I had an encounter with the doctor on duty that day and explained the situation. He did not seem to want to comply, so I requested a consultation with Louie's heart specialist. Doctors at the hospital had the consultation with Dr. Partele's associate who recommended that Louie be put back on the Amiodorone.

"Finally," I thought, "this issue is settled." I was wrong. More about the Amiodorone war later.

The days of waiting at the hospital in the waiting room most of the day were very long. Some of my friends and family wondered how I could handle the long hours between visits with Louie in ICU.

I can only say that I knew I was where God wanted me to be—in His will—and that this was my ministry at this time. As long as I walked in God's will, I knew He would give me the strength and peace I needed—and He did!

In addition to the comfort provided by God, I had a constant stream of visitors who sat with me many hours. My daughter Dana came every day during her lunch break and called me several times during the day to see if everything was all right or if I needed anything. My friend Jenifer Williams, who works at the hospital, came almost every day on her lunch break and again in the afternoons when she got off work. Her smiling face and comforting words and prayers were such a blessing. My dear friend Mac Swanson came so many times to sit with me for hours at the time. My friends Bud and Judy McLawhon made many trips to keep me company and check on Louie. My pastor, Grant Carter, came almost every day, even when his own father had open-heart surgery in the same hospital.

This is to name only a few who rallied around me to help me get through this crisis. So many people from my church, especially from my Sunday School class, and lifelong friends from Ayden came to visit. Each visitor and each visit was such a blessing. There were many, many phone calls during the day that also helped make the days shorter. The many cards and e-mail messages awaiting me at home each evening were also a great encouragement.

Friends would sometimes take me to lunch in the cafeteria or coffee shop. They usually offered to take me away from the hospital for a break from the routine there, but I hated to get too far away from the ICU unit. Louie's surgeon, Dr. Pendleton, came nearly every day to give me an update, and I was afraid I would miss seeing him. Also, I never knew when someone would need me to sign for another medical procedure. I wanted to be close at hand if I were needed for anything. Furthermore, I did not want to miss friends and family who were constantly stopping by for visits.

I was becoming very well acquainted with many of the other family members and friends of patients who were waiting with me. As I heard stories of their loved ones' crises, I often gave thanks that I was not in their place. I prayed with all those who shared their stories, and there were many who did. I also prayed for those I saw across the waiting room who seemed anxious but appeared to want privacy. I knew God was aware of their needs, so I just asked Him to be with them and their loved ones.

One of the ladies I met was Lacy. She had shared with me briefly in the waiting room that her husband Bennie had just undergone a Triple "A" procedure (repairing a major aneurysm on his aorta) like the one Louie had undergone a few years earlier. At the time Bennie was in Intermediate Care and was going home that day. She was curious about how long it had taken my husband to recover from the same procedure.

Lacy and Bennie went home, but after being home one day, Bennie was back in ICU. He had hemorrhaged and also had food coming out of his incision. Doctors did emergency surgery and learned that his bowel had been punctured during the initial surgery while he was being sewn up, and now they had to remove part of the bowel. A third surgery was required to remove still more of the bowel. Doctors had to leave him open this time to heal from the inside because he could not be sewn up again. Later he had another crisis with his heart and had to be shocked. It was a very close call for Bennie.

I learned that Lacy was a committed Christian, and we often prayed for each other's spouse. Many of her family members spent hours and hours in that waiting room, usually staying overnight and sleeping in the few recliners in the waiting room.

There was also Janet whose husband Lloyd was in ICU as a result of complications from surgery. I had just learned that after long stays in ICU under sedation, some patients develop what is called "ICU psychosis," where the patient is hallucinating. It turned out that Janet's husband eventually had this phenomenon as he began to wake up. He told Janet a whole scenario about the CIA bugging his room and the bulletin board having coded messages on it. He, like many of the patients in ICU, was trying to be weaned from the ventilator. I was learning that this was not always an easy process.

Another family had a wife/mother who had been in terrible wreck while driving a truck. She had sustained many broken bones and was in serious condition.

Terry was there for his 16-year-old daughter who had been severely injured in a wreck and was unresponsive in ICU. He had been there night and day for over 30 days without going back to his home in Rocky Mount.

Twenty-two-year-old Nick, who was the nephew of one of my former high school classmates, had been in an automobile accident and sustained serious brain damage. His family and fiancée were there night and day.

A young mother was in ICU. Her only child, an eight-year-old, had been killed in an automobile accident in which the mother was the driver. Just one day after the child's funeral, the mother had passed out and had been taken to Pitt Memorial where she required brain surgery due to a clot on her brain. Her family and many friends were there for her night and day. That family was on the prayer list of many area churches, including my own.

Another family was there for their 22-year-old son. He had just graduated from East Carolina University and had been shot at a party by someone who allegedly came in to rob the group. His family was told that he was paralyzed, and doctors were not sure if he would ever walk again.

Marlene was there for her husband who had colon cancer and had endured four surgeries. He had been in and out of ICU several times. She was very stressed and seemed so alone. Very few family members came to support her. I had several opportunities to share with her and to pray for her and her husband. Eventually, Marlene was told by doctors that she needed to invoke her husband's living will. What a difficult thing to have to do. Some of her husband's family resented Marlene's decision, which made it even harder. Eventually, her husband succumbed to the cancer.

A young marine was there with his wife. She had been through a supposedly routine operation at a military base hospital to remove her gallbladder. This young man believed the operation had been badly botched, and his wife had hemorrhaged. After being given 26 units of blood, she had been transferred from the military base to PCMH. Like so many others, he had been waiting with his wife for many days.

I saw another family dealing with the decision to take a loved one off life support. My heart ached for them and the extremely difficult decision they had to make.

A mother and father in their seventies were there constantly to be with their daughter who had been in a serious automobile accident.

A couple from the western part of the state were there because their son had been in a serious motorcycle accident. A local pastor shared with me that this couple was having a rough time financially because of the expense of staying in a motel. His church had taken an offering to help them with expenses.

These are just some of the stories. There were so many more. So many sick people and so many hurting family members were housed in a relatively small place. I knew that on other floors of the hospital there were even more stories. I don't think I had ever felt so much compassion for the sick and their families.

I prayed for all these people, and I prayed with many of them. I found most of them to be committed Christians, and their faith bolstered mine. There were a few who seemed not to have the faith to get them through, and it was my privilege to share with some of them about who God is in my life and how He was sustaining me and to pray that they might come to trust God with their lives and the lives of their loved ones.

There were so many special moments during these times of prayer and sharing when I felt that if God had allowed our crisis for no other reason than for me to have that brief interlude of prayer with someone, then it would have been worth it all. That may sound strange, but I know God is able to orchestrate where we are at any given point in our lives in order to make a difference. I don't know if anything I said to anyone made any difference, but I tried my best to be obedient when I felt God leading me to witness on His behalf. It was up to Him to do the rest.

Another person I had the opportunity to share with was Louie's good friend George. George is a nickname for a young Chinese friend whom Louie has known for about ten years. Louie more or less adopted George years ago, in his heart, and has helped him throughout the years with many things. For instance, Louie spent months helping George open his first restaurant in Kinston several years ago, and he had spent about six months prior to his surgery helping George open a Chinese buffet in our town of Ayden.

Louie did not do the physical work, but he helped George understand the English required to get the job done. He spent nearly every day for months keeping an eye on the progress of the refurbishing of the building where the new restaurant would be located.

George does not believe in God. Louie had given him a Chinese Bible years before and had shared his faith with him over the years. However, I had never had a very long conversation with George about his faith. I found it very difficult to communicate with him because of his limited understanding of English.

George loves Louie just like a father. He was totally distraught when he found out about Louie's illness. When he came to visit Louie at the hospital, he completely lost it after seeing him in ICU. I had to tell him, "George, you can't 'lose it' in front of Louie. Maybe he's not hearing what we are saying, but he may be. So we have to say only positive things in his presence." As a matter of fact, that was my personal rule for all who went into Louie's room. I did not want anyone to say anything about the seriousness of his condition or anything negative in his presence or comment on how long he had been in ICU. No one knew whether he could hear what we were saying or not, but I was not taking any chances. If he opened his eyes, I wanted him to see smiles.

After one of George's visits with Louie, he sat for some time with me in the waiting room, and I had a chance to share my faith with him. I also told him about a Chinese Bible study I had found in a church in Greenville where he could go to hear about God and Jesus in his own language. He actually agreed to go, much to my surprise, and he has been several times since then.

George invited me to stop by every evening for dinner at his restaurant in Ayden after I left the hospital. Obviously, I wasn't going to eat there every night, but I did stop by there every week or so to eat dinner and to update George. This provided me several opportunities to witness to George.

On one visit I as I was sharing with George, I asked him to go outside and take a look at all the stars. I asked him how he could see all that existed in the heavens and not believe that a divine Creator was responsible for such a magnificent plan! Everything that exists functions in such miraculous patterns, how could it be that this was just an accident as a result of a "big bang"? Besides that, what had existed to create a "big bang" in the first place? I pointed out to him that God was the Creator of everything, including man. He is the One who made man—even men like Mao and Buddha. They were, after all, just humans like ourselves with no power to create anything.

I shared with him that because we have all sinned we can never be worthy to be God's children. It was only by God's becoming man—Jesus—and dying on a cross as the ultimate sacrifice that we have any hope at all. We have to accept this wonderful gift in order to be forgiven and welcomed into God's kingdom. Since God is Spirit, a part of His precious Spirit comes to dwell inside us when we believe in Jesus and surrender our wills to Him.

When George told me one evening at the restaurant that he could not be as composed and strong as I was when he saw how sick Louie was, I explained to him that I was not walking in my own strength. I told him that what he was seeing was the strength God himself was providing me. I assured him that he, too, could have the same peace if he would give his heart to Jesus. This is just another "perk" that comes when we surrender to God. Obviously, our salvation is the most important thing—being able to spend eternity in Heaven with Him—but there are so many blessings that come to God's children in this life here on earth.

I also told George that God would go to any lengths to save him. While I did not believe that He sent this crisis to Louie since I know He loves His children too much to do that, I know that in His permissive will He may allow anything that would lead to saving a precious lost soul. It was possible that God had allowed this to happen so that George could hear and know the Truth.

I praise God for the opportunities He gave me to share with George. I hope one day he will surrender his heart to Jesus. He has since admitted that he did ask God to heal Louie. That is a beginning.

Chapter 6

Quiet Times

Rejoice always, pray without ceasing, in everything give thanks; for this is the will of God in Christ Jesus for you. (1 Thessalonians 5:16-18)

During the time I was with Louie at PCMH, I learned a few medical statistics I had never needed to know about before. I wrote in my group e-mail on April 6 that Louie's white blood count, which indicated his level of infection, was down to 11,000, with normal being between 4,000 and 10,000. He had come quite a ways from a white blood count of 27,000 a few days before due to pneumonia and a staph infection. I watched his monitors each time I was there to see what his blood pressure was, to check his heart rate, to see if his heart was beating rhythmically, and to check his oxygen level. I asked about his temperature and anything else I could think of.

I watched the ventilator and was beginning to learn a little about his oxygen percentage, volume, pressure, and respiration rate. When someone would come in from Respiratory, I would ask about changes that they made. I had learned that we need to breathe about 12 times a minute. Louie was nearly always breathing too fast. Often I would stand beside his bed and say, "Take a slow, deep breath. That's right. Breathe slow and easy." I would tell him that he was getting more oxygen by breathing slowly than when he breathed too fast. Even though Louie always appeared to be sleeping, sometimes I felt that he did slow down while I was doing this, but my visits were too short to make much of a difference.

The nurse told me on April 6 that Louie had squeezed her hand on command. While he did not do the same for me, I was excited that he was hearing and responding to the nurse's voice.

On this day the nurse had shaved Louie, which to me indicated progress. I felt that if she had time to do something so routine, Louie must be a little less critical. Every little positive sign gave me more hope and made me so thankful to God for the progress.

Doctors were telling me that they were beginning to try to wean Louie off the ventilator. They were constantly making adjustments on the ventilator to start this process. They did, however, continue to tell me that this would be a long process. It would probably be another couple of weeks after the vent weaning before he would wake up.

By April 9 doctors were wanting to do a bronchoscopy (camera on a tube inserted into the lung) to check for a recurrence of pneumonia. As with several other procedures he had, it was necessary for me to sign a permission form.

The next day I learned from the doctor that Louie did not have pneumonia this time, even though the doctor said he would have bet his house that he did. That was the good news. The bad news was that Louie had MRSA, which had been in the news so much in recent weeks. MRSA stands for methicillin-resistant Staphylococcus aureus. It's a strain of staph that's resistant to the broad-spectrum antibiotics commonly used to treat it.

I had read on the Web that about one-third of the population have MRSA in their noses or on their skin. Doctors told me that about 80 percent of the patients in the hospital test positive for MRSA. As long as the bacteria does not enter the body through a cut or wound, the carrier is said to be "colonized" but not infected. If MRSA gets into the body, it can be fatal.

Doctors assured me that Louie's MRSA was colonized in his nose and was not a major threat. They were treating it with a topical antibiotic. It did, however, mean that everyone visiting Louie would have to wear a protective plastic gown and latex gloves at each visit.

My greatest concern about this was that there was still the possibility that these bacteria could enter his body through a break in the skin, and he seemed to have so many, including the six puncture wounds from the laparoscopic surgery. Just as each step forward was a time for praise, each setback was a time for intercession on his behalf. I continued to keep my prayer warriors informed about Louie's progress and prayer needs.

Most of those who visited me at the hospital did not ask to see Louie. They knew he was usually sedated, so there was no opportunity to communicate with him. Those who did go in to see him were mostly family members and a few of our close friends who wanted to see him or pray for him. I was very protective of Louie during this time. He already had enough problems and was in isolation, so we had to don the plastic gowns and gloves every time we visited. I made sure every visitor used the antiseptic hand cleaner before and after visiting his room. Louie did not need another infection, and I certainly did not want anyone to take away something contagious from his room either.

I had really settled into my routine by now. My day at the hospital began around 9:15 or 9:30. I needed to get there early in order to find a decent parking place. Often I would stop in the coffee shop inside the main lobby for breakfast before going up to the fourth floor of the North Tower where the ICU was located.

Each day I spent the entire day in the waiting room except for the brief minutes with Louie in ICU. I normally love reading. Friends brought me a couple of books to help me pass the time, and I did read those books. However, for the most part, I found it very hard to concentrate on reading in the waiting room. I would take the newspaper with me each morning to read once I was settled in the waiting room. I would then work on the crossword puzzle for a little while before the first visit at 10:30. Although I love doing crossword puzzles and usually hate leaving one incomplete, I found it difficult to concentrate in this environment and rarely finished one while at the hospital.

Before Louie's crisis, I had routinely had a quiet time with the Lord spent in prayer and Bible study upon arising. This regular quiet time had started many years before. I recall how it all began.

I had always been an avid reader, and since being born again, I had chosen to read Christian books that would help me grow spiritually rather than novels and other works of fiction. These books had been very instrumental in helping me grow in my Christian faith. One of the most inspirational devotional books I enjoyed and learned from was *My Utmost for His Highest* by Oswald Chambers. I have read it over and over until the book is now quite worn, and I still keep it near my favorite chair and refer to it often. I have purchased many copies to give to friends because the book has blessed my life so much.

Even though I had acquired quite a library of Christian books that had taught me a lot, I still felt that I needed to focus on actual Bible study and have a specific prayer time each day. It seemed that mornings would be the best time for such consistent study, but I was at that time a "night" person. My mother always said when I was young that my eyes did not open until about three in the afternoon.

Although I never liked getting up early, I always got up early enough to get to work on time. Even in college I had always tried to sign up for 8 o'clock classes, preferring to get my classes finished early in the day, but it went against the grain, and I did not enjoy arising early.

I began sensing a need to spend more time with the Lord, based on what I heard pastors and authors saying about a need to do this, and had tried many times to institute a regular quiet time. It obviously had to be in the morning, since things were always hectic in the evenings in my household. With family activities, the television, phone calls, visitors, etc., the evenings never seemed to afford a quiet period long enough to engage in prayer for any length of time before bedtime. By the time things had settled down in the evenings, I was too tired to pray or study for any length of time.

I tried on many occasions over the years while my children were young to begin a regular quiet time by getting up early and studying the scriptures. Each time I tried, I would find myself reading and rereading the scriptures because I became so sleepy. I would pray and ask God to help keep me awake, but I would drift off to sleep in spite of my prayers. Ultimately, I would give up on my plan, only to try it again many months later when I would read a book by some

Christian author who stressed how important a daily devotional was. During those years I continued to find time to read many Christian books. However, I still felt I needed to spend a specific period each day studying my Bible and praying.

It is hard to say how many times I tried to have my own devotional time. Then one day things changed. Feeling an urgency to do so, I prayed once again and told the Lord that if He would keep me awake, I would get up each morning at 5 a.m. and spend time with Him. I set my clock, and on the first morning after that prayer, I got up, had a cup of coffee, and began reading my Bible.

It was an amazing morning! I had never appreciated how wonderfully quiet it was early in the morning before everyone else in the household awoke. The stillness was actually delicious. I began reading my Bible and was so engrossed in what I was reading that I hated to stop when it was 6:30 and time to get dressed for work.

I could not believe that I had stayed awake and alert and enjoyed that time of study and meditation and prayer so much. I was sure it was a fluke and would not happen the next day. Oh, ye of little faith!

The next day I repeated my activities and had a wonderful quiet time for an hour and a half. I was wide awake and thoroughly enjoyed every minute. Once again, I hated to stop when my time was up.

After many days of experiencing the same thing, I finally talked to God about what was going on. "Lord," I said, "I've prayed for you to change me from a night person to a morning person many, many times over the years, and you never answered that prayer before. Why have you answered it now?"

"My child," He said, "it's the first time you ever prayed it and *meant* it!"

I could not believe His words. All those times I had prayed it before, I didn't mean it? Surely I had. Then I reflected on what He was telling me, and the truth settled in my heart. All those times before when I had prayed for Him to keep me awake in order to have a quiet time, I was trying to do what everyone said I should do— pastors, writers, friends, etc. It was not until this most recent prayer that I had finally arrived at a time in my life where I truly wanted to spend time talking to my Father God. Wow! I could hardly contain myself at this revelation!

What I learned that day about prayer was life changing. I reviewed many of the other prayers I had said over the preceding years and realized that many of them had not been answered because I did not really *mean* them. I had said them with my mouth, but my heart was not in them. It was not until my heart desired the change that God was willing to answer my prayer.

In the years after God revealed this to me, I've prayed many prayers that started out asking God to change something or some attitude in my life, only to stop in the middle and say, "Wait a minute, God, I don't really mean that, do I? Let's start over. I know I should feel this way, but I don't. Help my heart to be sincere in what my mind knows is right. Look into my heart and clean it up as you see fit. Help me to know and desire your will, not mine."

My prayer times have remained a special time for me ever since. I discovered that God even began waking me up before my clock alarmed. I also discovered that He awakened me on Saturdays, Sundays, days off from work, holidays, etc. I, who had always been a sleepyhead in the morning, now awoke regularly at 5 a.m. while I was still working. Even in retirement I generally awaken at five, or earlier, and only rarely sleep until six.

Because of my ongoing morning prayer and study time for many years, it was surprising to me that during the time I was spending so many hours at the hospital, I was unable to focus on studying the Word. There was a Bible always in the car, as well as my Sunday School book, but for some reason I could not get into reading and studying in the hospital waiting room. Not that I didn't meditate a lot on His Word, for I certainly did. Countless scriptures were bouncing around in my head all the time. And I certainly was in prayer. No doubt about that.

While the realization that I was not studying did occur to me often, I never felt guilty about that period of lapse in my study time. Somehow, during all this crisis I had never felt closer to the Lord. He was so close to me every minute of every waking hour that I just didn't feel the need to study His Word as much as I felt the need to live His Word. I guess that I felt as if my entire day was a quiet time.

I trusted that my desire for actual Bible study would return when the hospital stay was over, and it did.

I always joined the chaplain and other visitors for prayer just prior to the first morning visit on weekdays. Some of those times in the prayer circle were awesome as we mentioned the names of our loved ones and named their special needs for the day. Occasionally the chaplain would ask if someone had something to share. On one of those occasions God impressed upon me to share what had happened the night I lost my ring and how God used that incident to show me His faithfulness in taking care of my husband.

Some of the Christians in the waiting room did not want to participate in the prayer circle each morning because the chaplain, we were told, was not permitted to use the name of Jesus. However, I always knew that my prayers were in His name, and I believed the others were also praying in His name. Whether it was said audibly or not didn't matter to me because I knew He read our hearts.

I continued to be blessed by God in so many other ways. He just kept meeting my needs, one by one. No detail seemed to have been neglected by Him.

Another example of God's provision was the long walk from the lobby to the North Tower where the ICU was located. At first I dreaded that long walk each morning. Also, I often ate lunch in the coffee shop, and since the coffee shop was located in the hospital lobby, that meant another long walk back to the hospital lobby for lunch. Later I came to realize that the long walk to the front of the hospital was the only exercise I was getting, and I decided I needed to make that long stroll as often as possible. At first it had seemed like a mile to walk, but the longer I stayed at the hospital, the shorter the walk became. Sometimes I would just take a stroll to the front of the hospital or walk a visitor to the front door for the exercise. I was able to thank God for the walk because I knew it was good for me to exercise a little after sitting so much during the day. God thinks of everything to meet our needs.

God was also providing the energy I needed each day to endure the long hours of waiting. Usually after the 6 p.m. visit, I would go home unless someone else came to visit. There was one final visit allowed at 8:30, but if I stayed for that visit, it meant I was arriving home after dark and getting to bed much later. I had decided that if all was going well, I would leave in time to arrive home before dark.

While I was at the hospital each day, I never recall feeling exhausted. Once I left each afternoon, I would begin to feel the tiredness creeping into my body on the 15-minute drive home. By the time I stopped for a bite to eat or fixed myself a snack at home, I was feeling exhausted. As soon as I settled in at home, I sat down and sent my e-mail for the day to my praying friends. Each evening I would think that I could stay up a while, but each evening I had to go to bed as soon as I sent my e-mail, read my messages, and returned phone calls. Unless I received a phone call, this meant I was heading to bed about 8:30 most evenings and asleep by 9:00. As soon as I was in bed, I was asleep.

I arose each morning about five, or occasionally earlier. After taking a shower, making the bed, having my cup of coffee, taking care of laundry, doing other household chores, paying the bills, etc., it was time to head to the hospital. I always awoke feeling rested and anxious to get back to the hospital.

This may sound extremely boring to the average reader, but anyone who is walking in God's will can attest to the fact that there can be perfect peace and even joy in this walk. Each day I felt so much gratitude that God was taking care of Louie and that He was sustaining me, I could not keep from feeling great joy.

Chapter 7

God Hears Our Prayers

*Every good gift and every perfect gift is from above, and
comes down from the Father of lights, with whom there is
no variation or shadow of turning. (James 1:17)*

By April 12, Louie had been in ICU three weeks. The previous
day doctors had reduced the percentage of oxygen he was
getting to the minimum amount they usually provide vent patients.
The staff said this was the beginning of the weaning process to get
him off the ventilator. Also, the nurses had reduced his sedation,
and his eyes were open more that day. Yet he was still not awake
enough to show recognition, and his breathing was still rapid. One
of the doctors told me he believed that the increased breathing rate
was due to anxiety Louie was experiencing as he began to come off
sedation, which was what I had thought all along.

By now I knew the worst of the pain from his initial surgery
should have passed, and again I was grateful that at least he had not
had to endure that pain.

I was continuing to feel such gratitude for all the support I was
receiving from our friends. On Sunday, April 13, I updated my
friends and family about Louie's progress. Here is the last part of
the e-mail message I sent that day:

Thanks to each of you for your prayers, calls, and visits! You will never know how much they have meant to me! God is so good to give us loving family and friends who support us when we're down and rejoice with us in the good times!

Those of you who have been able to visit me in the hospital have probably already heard me say this, but the others on this mailing list may not be aware of how mightily God is using this difficult time to work to our good. Many of you know that Romans 8:28 is one of my favorite verses. It says, "All things work together for good to them that love the Lord and are the called according to His purpose." I have seen this proven true over many years, and it continues to be true today.

This situation with Louie has certainly not been easy, but I have felt such an outpouring of love and prayer over us that I feel as if I'm in a bubble of peace. I cannot begin to describe the strength I have experienced as a result of your prayers and God's grace. He has always been there for me through every trial, and He continues to be with me now. He is ever faithful and loving and caring, and His peace passes all my understanding. I know that I can trust Him with every concern I have.

While I do not know everything God is doing in this situation to work it "all" for our good, I do see many of the evidences of this truth. While spending the long hours in the waiting room each day, I have encountered so many hurting people who have family members and friends in ICU. Since each patient is critical, we have quickly become like family members ourselves as we share our ups and downs. I have had the opportunity to pray with so many of these people and to witness to some of them who do not have a relationship with God. This opportunity would not have occurred if we had not been placed in this situation. Also, as I hear what others' loved ones are going through, I feel blessed that my situation is not as bad as theirs. I feel encouragement, too, as some of the patients improve and move to other units.

I see my own faith growing through this testing, and God is teaching me some valuable lessons. I'm so thankful that He loves me enough to keep working on me!

It is hard to explain how in the middle of a storm like this crisis, I can feel such a sweet peace that only the Lord can provide.

Again, thank you for your love and concern and prayers. I'm sure it is because of your prayers that I have been able to rest each night and feel refreshed at the beginning of each day!

Keep praying! God is sooooooooooooooo good!

On Sunday, April 13, I sent this brief message:

Louie remains about the same. His vital signs all seem to be very good. One very important encouragement today was that he was more nearly awake than I have seen him. There was even a brief moment when there was a glimmer of recognition in his eyes! The nurse saw it too, so I wasn't just imagining it. The nurse only gave him half a dose of pain medicine this afternoon, which allowed him to keep his eyes open in the afternoon. When his brother Robert and sister-in-law Debra visited at 6:00, they were very encouraged that he was more alert.

Keep praying!

Monday, April 14, was my birthday, and there was good news to make my day. I wrote to my friends

God is soooooo good! Yesterday I prayed for a glimmer of recognition from Louie, and, as you know, I got it! Today on the way to the hospital I thanked God again for that answered prayer, and then I apologized to the Lord that I am so greedy, but today I really wanted more than a glimmer! Guess what! You're right! I got what I prayed for!

Louie was very much more alert today and made eye contact nearly the whole time I was with him for my visits. I can tell he is still confused and anxious, but he is making eye contact with me and others. Praise the Lord!

I realize that it will still be a long haul until Louie is completely recovered, but I am so thankful for every little step in the right direction. Thank you again for every prayer lifted on behalf of Louie. Please pray that he can make this transition to total wakefulness as easily as possible.

What a perfect birthday present this has been for me today! As I said before, God is so good!

My friends Bud and Judy McLawhon had taken me out for lunch that day to celebrate my birthday. After my last visit that evening, friends Cliff and Cathy Cahoon and their daughter Ellen had taken me out for dinner at an Italian restaurant near the hospital. They had also invited Dana and Jansen and my sister-in-law Debra to share in the festivities, complete with birthday cake and gifts.

The following day Dana was very excited on her visit when her dad smiled at her. It is so amazing how excited one can get at such a simple gesture when actions typically taken for granted have been missing so long. I made a mental note to remember to be more thankful for small things I had always taken for granted before.

I wrote to Eric a couple of days later that his dad was mostly very sleepy during my visits, but on occasion he would be more alert. He always became very agitated when he wanted to tell me something, but he couldn't talk because of the trach; and I couldn't figure out what he needed.

As soon as I thought Louie was awake enough to understand what I was saying, I whispered in his ear, "God has promised that He will never forsake you, and neither will I." I was not sure if he heard or understood, but I desperately wanted him to know that I would be with him every step of the way. As he drifted in and out of consciousness, I wondered if he felt deserted when he awoke alone in his room. I often tried to reassure him that I was just a few steps away when I had to leave after my short visits.

Louie's CT scan of his abdomen at this time did not show any problems, and he was off antibiotics by now. They were still trying to wean him from the ventilator, but when he became more alert, he became agitated. This led to an increased breathing rate. I likened it to a Catch 22. If he could just wake up enough to really understand that medically he was out of his crisis, perhaps he would be less anxious and could get off the vent. However, waking up and being unable to speak due to the trach was alarming to him, leading to rapid breathing. It was a waiting game to find a balance between the meds and the vent that would allow him to be completely awake.

In the early days of Louie's struggle, I had been most concerned about the damage to his body and infections. I never dreamed how hard it was going to be to get him breathing on his own.

At least he was beginning to be responsive to some of our questions, but he was still somewhat confused and very frustrated with the trach and the feeding tube, which was still in his nose. The nurse had removed his restraints, and as he began to move his arms a little, the natural thing to do was to pull on his tubes, so he did—removing his feeding tube.

Visits were like a rollercoaster ride. Some days were good; some were not as good. One day I observed that Louie's breathing rate was up to 62 breaths a minute, when the normal would have been 12 breaths a minute. He was nearly panting. I did not leave his room until someone came in and gave him more meds. In just a few minutes his respiration rate was down to 13, and I could breathe a sigh of relief. Later that day, they did another bronchoscopy to check his lungs and to remove the junk accumulated in his bronchial tubes due to his excessive secretions.

Chapter 8

Forgiveness

Let all bitterness, wrath, anger, clamor, and evil speaking
be put away from you, with all malice. And be kind to one
another, tenderhearted, forgiving one another, even as God
in Christ forgave you. (Ephesians 4:31-32)

There were other battles along the way. I was very concerned about Louie's being given so much Ativan. I realized he needed to be kept sedated in the initial days of his crisis because of the pain from the surgery and the trauma to his body from going into shock. However, it seemed that each time he was becoming a little more alert, he would be given more sedation.

I would always question everything that was going on. I really tried to be as tactful as I could, but I needed to know what they were doing to Louie and why. Louie's surgeon had turned him over to the ICU team of hospitalists at the outset of the crisis, even though he continued to check on his progress daily. With different doctors rotating on and off shifts, no one doctor seemed to have a plan laid out that told me where we were going and how long it would take to get there. I was very anxious to see him awake and to know that he was really okay.

It was frustrating not to see one of the attending physicians each day. Usually the only way I saw one was to request of the nurse that I speak to whoever was on duty that day. Dr. Pendleton usually came by the waiting room each day, but he was not one of the ones who were actually treating Louie. Furthermore, on one occasion I mentioned to the ICU doctor something Dr. Pendleton had told me, and the doctor informed me that if I had questions, I should ask the ICU doctors. He said that Dr. Pendleton had released Louie to their care, and they were the ones who knew what was going on. Wow! That would have been okay if I could have spoken to one of these attending physicians every day. When I did get to speak to one, it would be as he or she was making rounds. I'd get maybe 2 or 3 minutes outside Louie's door to ask my questions.

For the most part, Louie had apparently been given excellent care by his doctors and his nurses. They seemed very efficient and concerned about what was going on. However, in the days to come, I had a very troubling experience with one of the nurses.

James had been one of my favorite nurses. He seemed very caring and very attentive. As mentioned before, I did ask lots of questions of his nurses. James seemed to be very patient when responding to me. One of the things I continued to ask about was how much sedation he was getting and why.

On one particular day, I mentioned to James as I left Louie's room that Louie seemed more agitated that day than usual. He said, "Well, I didn't give him his meds this morning because I wanted you to see how he gets when he doesn't get them."

I could not believe my ears! "Listen," I managed to say with a calm voice even though I had found this very shocking, "you don't have to show me anything. I want you to give my husband whatever he needs."

I was very upset as I headed back to the waiting room. I mulled this event in my mind for the next two hours before my next visit. I also prayed for God to help me have a forgiving heart and to give me the wisdom to handle this situation in a Christlike manner. The issue was not over for me.

After my next visit, I told James that I needed to talk to him. He started to come inside the room where Louie was, thinking perhaps that I wanted him to do something for Louie, and I said, "No, let's talk outside his room."

My words to him went something like this. "James, I did not feel good after our last conversation. It really bothered me. I want you to know that what I want for my husband is the very best possible care he can get. When I ask questions, I am not suggesting that I know what he needs, but I do want to know what is going on and why. He is not able to ask for himself, and I am now my husband's advocate. I certainly don't want him to suffer because I ask questions."

James apologized, and I accepted his apology. Before I left, I said one other thing. "James, I'm sure you've seen hundreds of patients just like this."

He nodded his head in assent. "Well, that may be routine for you, but I want you to know one thing. This is the only husband I have, and I want him to be treated by you as if he were your father."

The next day as I went in to visit Louie, the attending physician for the day came into Louie's room. I cannot recall if I had ever met him before that day or not. He did not greet me or ask how I was doing. He started his conversation by saying, "Mrs. Tyndall, you need to leave the doctoring to us. We know what we're doing."

I was completely floored! "Dr. Byrd," I said, "I want to assure you that I don't have any medical training, and I have no idea how my husband needs to be treated. I have to trust that the professionals know what is best for him. However, I do want you to know that I ask a lot of questions because I want to know what is going on. Furthermore, as soon as Louie is better, he's going to want to know what went on." Since I had not questioned this doctor, I could only assume that James or another nurse had shared with this doctor about questions I asked.

Part of my message to my prayer partners on April 18 was

This process [Louie's recovery] is very frustrating. Added to that, I had to deal with a rude doctor today and a rude nurse yesterday. This did not help my stress level. As you continue to pray for Louie, please pray for me to have patience.

Later, when Dr. Pendleton called me out of the waiting room to update me on Louie, I shared the nurse story and the doctor story with him. "Dr. Pendleton," I said, "it's very hard being a family member spending hours and hours in this waiting room not knowing what is going on. Our visits are very infrequent and very short. I don't have the medical training to understand very much of what is going on, but this is my husband who is being cared for, and I need to know what is going on. I'm sorry the doctors and nurses feel intimidated when I ask questions. I have great respect for doctors and other medical personnel and all the training they have been through to prepare themselves. However, there is no reason for them to be rude to me or take out their frustrations with me on my husband."

He apologized for his associate and said he would speak to the doctor who had been so rude. He also said if I gave him the name of the nurse, he would speak to him. I told him that would not be necessary. I felt I had let the nurse know how I felt. If he wanted to talk to his associate, that would be fine. However, I suggested, he might in general explain to all the nurses on duty that those loved ones spending anxious hours in the waiting room deserved some respect.

On an earlier occasion I had felt that Dr. Pendleton also became very impatient with me. Since Louie had not awakened after so many days, I asked him on a couple of occasions if he thought a brain scan would be a good idea.

"I'm going to order a brain scan today for him!" he said emphatically. "Even though there are risks involved with this procedure, I'm going to order it."

"Wait a minute," I said. "I don't want you to do anything that would put my husband at risk."

"Well," he said, "you've mentioned a CT scan three times."

"Dr. Pendleton," I said, "I only mentioned it because you told me a few days after he went into ICU that if he didn't wake up soon, you were going to order a brain scan. If you don't think it's warranted, please don't do anything to jeopardize Louie's health."

I thought the matter was ended and that there would be no brain scan. However, the next day I mentioned my concern about possible brain damage to the attending physician, and he said a brain scan had already been done on April 2, as ordered by Dr. Pendleton. No one had yet given me the results, but this doctor looked it up on the computer just outside Louie's door right away, showed it to me, and said, "Everything looks fine. There doesn't appear to be any obvious problem with the brain."

This made me feel much better, but I was a little hurt with the manner in which Dr. Pendleton had spoken to me. Later, when I was sharing with Dr. Pendleton about the rudeness of his associate and the nurse, I hoped he remembered the incident about the CT scan and took my comments to heart.

There was one other event that happened at PCMH that bothered me. A family member, who is a physical therapist herself, had expressed concern to the nurse that Louie was not getting physical therapy and that his position was not being changed often enough. Soon after this, I went in one day to find Louie in a bed that converted to a chair-like sitting position. I was thrilled to see him sitting almost completely upright.

On my next visit, two hours later, I found Louie in the same position. I was concerned that he may have been left in the upright position for the whole two hours, thinking that may have been a bit too long.

When I went in two hours after this, my sister-in-law Debra was with me. Once again Louie was sitting upright. I now wondered if he had been left upright for four hours. I asked the nurse, James (yes, the same James), if Louie had been allowed to stay upright for the whole four hours, and he said no, that he had not been upright the entire time.

The next day Louie's legs had to be totally bandaged because all the fluid he had accumulated in his body had begun to seep out the skin on his legs. The nurse on duty this day said his legs needed to be kept up to prevent the fluid from accumulating in them. I did not see Louie in the upright position again. He continued to have problems with his legs after that. Since they were bandaged, I could not see them, but I later learned that they developed some sores as a result of this problem.

Chapter 9

Seeking God's Wisdom

If any of you lacks wisdom, let him ask of God, who gives
to all liberally and without reproach, and it will be given to
him. (James 1:5)

Louie's condition continued about the same for the next few days. He was usually sleeping when I visited him. On April 19 doctors did an ultrasound of his legs, and it did not show any blood clots. Apparently, the one he had when he entered the hospital had dissolved, and no others had developed. We were so grateful for this bit of news.

His surgeon told me he believed the process of weaning Louie off the vent was going to take a long time. He informed me that there was an optional plan available. He told me about a hospital called LifeCare, which was located in Rocky Mount, that focused on aggressively weaning people from vents. They also provided physical therapy, which was unavailable to ICU patients at Pitt Memorial. The only therapy given in ICU was some range of motion exercises given by nurses. The doctor thought I might want to consider moving Louie to this facility in Rocky Mount.

Dr. Pendleton assured me that I could leave Louie at Pitt Memorial and they would continue to treat him. He indicated that it would probably be at least another six weeks, although no one could possibly know for sure how long it would take. He said the decision was mine, and I should choose whatever was more convenient for me.

Obviously, staying at Pitt Memorial would be more convenient for me. I would only have to travel 10 miles versus the 55-mile trip to Rocky Mount. My family and all my friends were just a few miles away, but if we moved to Rocky Mount, it would be more difficult for everyone to visit.

My first thought, however, had to be Louie's care. If the doctor thought Louie could get well in half the time at this other hospital and also believed LifeCare was a cleaner facility where Louie would be less likely to get another infection, it seemed that I had to give this option some serious thought.

I knew absolutely nothing about LifeCare. I'd never even heard of it before. I wrote to my friends and family that night

We could use a miracle right now. If Louie would wake up and be responsive, I would not have to make a decision regarding LifeCare. However, if he does not improve this week, I am seriously considering the move. It certainly will not be very convenient for his family since the facility is about an hour away, but we want what is best for Louie. I can't imagine waiting six more weeks with no assurance that the hospital's efforts will be successful. Please pray for God to give me the wisdom to make the best decision in this situation.

A bright spot in all that was going on occurred about this time. I had not been available to spend time with my only grandchild, Jansen, in weeks. I wrote in my daily message

This afternoon Dana stayed at the hospital and let me keep Jansen. While I didn't have a real need to get out of the hospital, I was in need of a "Jansen fix"! He is such a sweetie pie, and I haven't had but a few moments with him in weeks. I have been delighted to have him this afternoon. He is sitting at my feet now with all the toys at Nana's house strewn in the den floor! He will be spending the night with me, and tomorrow I plan to attend early church and take Jansen. It seems like years since I was in church, and I really need to be there.

Two days later I made an early morning trip to Rocky Mount to visit LifeCare and to learn more about their operation. I e-mailed my friends

I visited the LifeCare Hospital in Rocky Mount Monday morning before going to see Louie. The facility is small — just 40 beds. Patients transferred there must spend at least the first 24 hours in Observation (their ICU). I didn't see anything negative. I have heard reports of successes from former patients. Since the doctors at PCMH are recommending that Louie be transferred there, I have decided that this will be the next step. There is currently not a room at LifeCare, but Louie has already been referred by the hospital and is second on the waiting list. Once LifeCare offers me a space, I will make the final decision. Unless there is a dramatic change before a room opens up at LifeCare, this will be the route we take.

After much prayer, I had decided to move Louie to Rocky Mount unless he made a startling change soon. My understanding was that he would stay one or possibly two nights in the Observation Unit, which accommodated only five patients, until he could be evaluated. Then he would be moved into a room where I would be able to stay with him day and night. It would not be so bad having to drive back and forth to Rocky Mount only a couple of times a week to take care of things at home. Even though my friends would not find it convenient to visit there, I would be with Louie and would not be alone. At least this was the plan.

The rest of my e-mail on April 21 tells more of how I was feeling at this time, what was going on with Louie, and the wonderful experience I had when I was able to be in my church for the first time in weeks.

The nurse on duty Monday had changed Louie's oxygen volume when I arrived at 10:30. She said she couldn't stand to see him so agitated. She had tried some meds, which didn't work. Once she adjusted his oxygen, he calmed down and was resting well. She believes he was anxious and breathing fast because he wasn't getting enough oxygen! Wonder why someone else didn't think of that? Since the number showing his oxygen level was very good (98-100), I assumed everything was okay there.

They put in a PICC [peripherally inserted central catheter — a form of intravenous access] line yesterday, which can stay in longer and is less likely to be the source of an infection. I presume they will be removing the existing central line, which has already been in as long as it should.

I thank God every day for his love and grace and mercy in bringing Louie this far. I continue to ask God to restore him to his former level of health. I have not prayed for God to give him perfect healing because I believe perfect healing occurs when we go home to be with the Lord! Right now, I don't want "perfect healing." I just want a temporary healing that will allow Louie to enjoy a quality life here a little longer!

God is continuing to work mightily in my life through this crisis. Those of you who were in my church Sunday morning must know how blessed I was by the special prayer our pastor, Grant Carter, had for Louie and me and my family at the beginning of the service. Those present gathered around me as Grant prayed the most beautiful prayer! I was so touched and blessed by this prayer. It was also wonderful just to be in church once again and see my church family. To top it off, Grant preached a fantastic sermon, as he always does! How uplifting! Can't imagine why anyone would choose not to be a part of a church family like mine!

As you pray for Louie today, please remember all the other hurting family members in that waiting room! There are so many sad, hurting people there. Yet I see small prayer groups gathered all during the day. I hear many testimonies of faith in God. I am encouraged as I see other Christians trusting God with their loved ones! I was personally blessed to have pastors Grant, Bill Gay, and David Langley visit me yesterday and to have each of them pray with me—along with a bunch of other friends who are not pastors, but whose prayers I know are also with me! This was not an unusual day, but a typical day! Can you see how blessed I am?

God bless you today. Sorry I ran on so long!

Chapter 10

LifeCare

*You will keep him in perfect peace, Whose mind is stayed
on You, Because he trusts in You. (Isaiah 26:3)*

L ouie continued to remain pretty sleepy on my next few visits,
even though I was told he had not been given any sedation.
The ICU doctor, Dr. Tosky, who was on duty at the time, told me he
had given Louie a different drug, Haldol, which he thought would
be more helpful. I checked the new drug on the Web that night and
wrote to my e-mail buddies that it sounded pretty scary to me and I
hoped the doctor knew what he was doing.

The next day Louie was a little more alert. His eyes were open
and followed me as I arrived at his room and moved about. He was
sitting with his upper body upright and looked very relaxed. His
breathing rate was good as were his other numbers.

I wrote to my friends on April 23

I learned from the nurse that his meds had been changed
again. When I asked the doctor why they had taken him off
Haldol, he said he had learned from the pharmacist that it
was not compatible with Amiodorone, which Louie needs
to keep his heart in rhythm! Hello! Wouldn't you think they
would have checked BEFORE giving it to him? Well, I

wasn't too thrilled with Haldol when I read about all the side effects, so I was actually relieved.

At any rate, they have changed it now. They will only be giving him pain/sedation meds if he becomes too agitated. Today he seemed relaxed and actually was responsive to a couple of my questions. At my last visit, he even smiled at me! Good news!

Today they switched his trach to a longer model to help him with secretions.

I also learned today that a room may become available at LifeCare at the end of this week. I'm ready to move him! I'll keep you posted when we move.

I'm so tired and sleepy when I get home that my notes may sound like blithering. Please consider my mental state and overlook any typos and weird grammar.

I love each of you and appreciate your concern so much. Thank you for your prayers. They keep me going!

The next day Louie was more alert. His brother Robert and sister-in-law Debra were very pleased that he was so responsive when they visited at 4:30 and 6:00. The nurse told us they had planned to move Louie to Intermediate Care on this day, but there was no room available. We were still waiting for a room to be available at LifeCare as well.

Since Louie was more alert, I told him about the plan to move to Rocky Mount. He did not seem upset about this news, and that was a good thing. I was hoping that he comprehended what I was talking about. He had smiled several times during the day, which made my day.

On April 25 I sent the following message to my online contacts:

Today was another "sleepy" day for the most part. Louie had been given sedation early this morning. It didn't wear off until my 6 p.m. visit. At that time he was fairly alert.

They did not move him to Intermediate today because there was no bed. There was also no word from the hospital in Rocky Mount yet, so we're just on hold.

I spoke to one of Louie's doctors this morning—Dr. Tosky, whom I like a lot—and he thinks Louie is doing very well. He has no medical problems that we know of except the need to get off the ventilator and to receive physical therapy. They are turning down the respiratory support gradually and forcing Louie to breathe more on his own as long as he doesn't get agitated. He was breathing very well today even with these new settings, so I think that is a very good sign.

When I say he has no medical problems, I'm aware that he will have to learn to tolerate food again and he has to get off the urinary tract catheter, etc., but he doesn't have any indications of infection or other medical issues that we know of.

I am very, very thankful for every little improvement. Please know that I am aware of how awesome God is, and while things don't always move as quickly as I might prefer, God is still in control. His timing for each step will be perfect, and I'm still trusting Him. His grace is sufficient, and I praise Him every day that He is so trustworthy! His peace truly does pass understanding!

Thanks to each one again for every single prayer. God is hearing and honoring your prayers!

On Saturday, April 26, Louie was a little more responsive and actually mouthed a few words to us. I thought this was a wonderful, positive sign. After my last visit for the day, I went home with the intention of keeping my grandson for the night. However, about 7:30 I received a call from the hospital that Louie was being moved to Intermediate Care in an hour or so. What great news.

I had Dana pick up Jansen, wrote a quick e-mail to my friends about the good news, and headed back to the hospital to spend the night in the room with Louie.

That night and Sunday night Louie was awake pretty much all night, and I didn't get much sleep either. It seems that when one has been in ICU so long, he/she loses a sense of day and night. Adjusting to a routine of being awake in the daytime and sleeping at night takes a little time. Obviously, someone was constantly coming into the room to check on Louie, which was a good thing. I wanted him to get all the care necessary to make him well again. Both of us did nap a little during the day on Sunday.

Part of the time when Louie was awake he was responsive. Other times he was very frustrated that he could not communicate. Sunday night he pulled his feeding tube out. Once it was reinserted, he had to have X-rays of his stomach to make sure the tube was correctly placed without a twist in it. During the early morning hours, this process took place three times. Each time they came in to make an X-ray, I had to leave the room. After the X-ray, they would leave, check the X-ray, find it was not correctly placed. The nurse would reposition the tube, and the X-ray technician would return to make another X-ray. Finally, after the third episode, the feeding tube was positioned correctly. This was yet another reason why it was so hard to sleep.

For the next couple of days Louie remained alert most of the time. At other times, especially at night, he seemed to be in another world. Since he could not speak, I didn't have a clue what he was thinking during those times. I would see him looking strangely at the room or the frame holding his vent tubes. He had a particular fascination with the light on his finger from the device (pulse oximeter) measuring the oxygen saturation level in his blood. I called this his "ET" finger, after the movie character. He would hold it up and look at it wonderingly.

Most of the time he was responsive to my questions requiring a "yes" or "no" answer. Whenever he tried to communicate with me otherwise, he would become very frustrated because neither I nor the nurses nor visitors could read his lips. I was as frustrated as he was because I so much wanted to know what he was trying to tell me.

I tried giving him a pen and pad, but he could not write. His hands were very tremulous, and his attempt was no more than a scribble. To him it may have seemed like writing, but it was only a wavy line on the page. I tried pointing to letters of the alphabet on a chart in the hospital room and sometimes reciting letters of the alphabet, thinking he could nod at the correct letters and spell out what he wanted to tell me, but that did not work either. I named every part of his anatomy to see if there was something hurting or a limb that needed to be moved. Nothing worked. The next time I sent an e-mail to my contact list, I asked for suggestions from anyone who could come up with a plan for better communication.

Louie was having lots of lung secretions and was constantly coughing. When he would cough a lot, it would set off the ventilator alarms. Most of the time the nurse would have to come in and suction him, which was not a fun process, but it did help him breathe easier after the process. The nurses and respiratory therapists were constantly in and out of the room, day and night.

Earlier nurses had told me Louie's weight had increased 50-60 pounds due to his fluid buildup. His arms, legs, and abdomen were huge. His arms had earlier seeped fluid in a few spots and had to have bandages to absorb these secretions. He was beginning to move his arms more, which helped with the swelling in them. However, as soon as he became less active, the swelling would return. Now, as mentioned before, his legs had to be completely wrapped with bandages for the same reason.

At this time, Louie was running a low-grade fever, and we were told that he had a slight urinary tract infection. This was supposedly the only infection he had, so this was not expected to be a problem with his transfer to LifeCare whenever a room became available. He had been given another transfusion on April 29 for chronic anemia.

On Wednesday afternoon, April 30, we finally got the word that a room was available at LifeCare in Rocky Mount. I was given a copy of his final discharge papers that summarized his medical problems and treatments at Pitt Memorial. I noted that his recent urine cultures had come back positive for Pseudomonas, an infection caused by a bacterium that can attack any part of the body and is particularly prevalent among patients in hospitals. He also was being treated for possible C. diff (short for Clostridium difficile colitis, a colon infection that causes diarrhea). This was the first time I had heard of these two infections.

I was anxious about Louie's actual transfer to Rocky Mount. I had been told that the EMS vehicle he was to be transported in contained all the necessary life support equipment to safely move him to LifeCare. I stayed with him until the EMS team arrived. While they were preparing to transfer Louie, I left and headed to Rocky Mount in order to be there when he arrived.

Once I arrived at LifeCare, I expected the ambulance to be close behind. It seemed I waited at least an hour before they finally arrived at 7 p.m. By then I was becoming quite anxious. I had not looked forward to the actual transfer itself, knowing that it was going to be a bumpy ride. All sorts of other possibilities had also crossed my mind — accidents, vehicle breakdowns, medical complications. I was very relieved when I finally learned that he had arrived and was being taken to the Observation Unit. I could not see him until he was settled there, but I finally was permitted to visit with him in his new location about 8 o'clock.

Louie appeared to have weathered the trip all right. Once again I tried to explain to him where he was and why he was there. I was pretty sure he had been sedated for the ride, so I wasn't sure if anything I said was understood.

Since the Observation Unit is equivalent to the ICU, I was only permitted to visit a short time before I had to leave for the drive back home to Ayden. Honestly, I still had some misgivings as to whether I had done the right thing by moving him to Rocky Mount. However, I had prayed about it, and all I could do was to continue to entrust Louie to God and ask Him to take care of my husband.

I came home, wrote a quick e-mail message to my friends about the day's events, and got to bed about 11 p.m. Hopefully, Louie would only be in the Observation Unit a day or two, and once he was moved to his own room, I would be able to stay with him all the time. I was really looking forward to that. He had been at Pitt Memorial for a little over six weeks and in ICU nearly five of those weeks. I anticipated that in a few weeks at LifeCare he would be weaned from the ventilator and be moved back to Greenville for more physical therapy in Rehab at Pitt Memorial. Doctors at Pitt had told me to expect Louie to need weeks of therapy — three days for every day spent in ICU — in Rehab. Knowing Louie's disposition and determination, I believed he would not need as long a period of therapy as they predicted, but I assumed he would definitely need some. Even though this was still going to mean weeks of recovery, I could see the light at the end of the tunnel.

PART 2

THE SECOND LEG OF THE JOURNEY

Chapter 11

Overcoming Fear

*Be strong and of good courage, do not fear nor be afraid
of them; for the LORD your God, He is the One who goes
with you. He will not leave you nor forsake you.*
(Deuteronomy 31:6)

My sleep was abruptly interrupted by the ringing of the phone at 2:30 on Thursday morning! One never expects good news at this hour, and my heart was pounding as I answered the phone. Caller ID revealed that it was LifeCare calling, and I instantly was aware that the news could not be good. I was right.

The nurse on duty was calling to tell me that during the night Louie's temperature had spiked to 104 degrees, his blood pressure had gone down to half of what was normal, and he was nauseous. She told me they had put a cooling sheet on him and that at the time his temperature was down to 99 and the blood pressure was back up to a safe range. I told her that I would leave immediately for the hospital, but she said that Louie was now stable and that they had started him on another antibiotic. If his condition should worsen, they would transport him back to Pitt Memorial, but for now she said they could handle the problem. She said there was no need for me to come because I would not be able to see him until the regular visiting hour at 10 that morning anyway. She just wanted me to know what was going on. They were running tests to try to find the source of the infection. I was told I could call the nurses' station at any time to check on his condition.

My heart sank! What had I done? I remember writing in my notebook later that day—in shorthand so that no one else could likely read it—the question, "Have I brought my husband to LifeCare to die?"

After the phone call, I called family members to alert them to what had happened and to request their prayers. Obviously, there was not going to be any more sleep at this point. I felt that we were right back where we had been six weeks ago at PCMH. It seemed it would be forever before I could travel to Rocky Mount to check on Louie for myself. All I knew to do was to pray. At a time like this, God is the only One who can bring comfort and peace. Once again I had to commit Louie into His care, knowing He would do whatever was best. I also needed His reassurance that I had made the right choice in moving Louie to LifeCare.

Since I knew sleep would not be possible with this latest news, I turned on the television in my bedroom to help me focus on something besides my concerns. There was an interesting program about an archeological study that was made to try to determine where Moses crossed the Red Sea with the Israelites. After watching it for just a few minutes, God did reassure me that He was still in control! He reminded me that if He could handle the parting of the Red Sea to deliver His people, He could still handle my needs. He is so wonderful! His peace truly does pass understanding.

Around 5:30 that morning I called LifeCare, and Louie's nurse said he was resting. They had done blood cultures to determine the source of the infection, but they would take a few days to develop. They had also changed his Foley catheter, which was apparently overdue for a change. Since he still had a urinary tract infection, they thought this was the most likely culprit. They were also concerned about a possible infection in his PICC line, which had been inserted very recently at Pitt Memorial. I hoped it would not be necessary to change that line again. Any procedure like that ran possible risks.

Before I headed to Rocky Mount that morning, I e-mailed our friends to tell them what was going on and to ask them to be continue in prayer for Louie. It was a long drive that morning and a long wait before I was finally able to see Louie in the Observation Unit. When I had visited LifeCare for the first time, the only thing I had found troubling about the facility was the size of the Observation Unit. As I mentioned before, it would only accommodate five patients.

There was a common patient area in the middle of the unit accommodating three patients and two separate small rooms, one on either end of the common area. There was a nurses' station in the common area. What had troubled me was that the three patients in the common area were so close together. There was no privacy except for curtains that could be drawn to separate them. Staff had explained to me that they used the two individual rooms, which had see-through glass windows, for patients with infections.

While I was sorry Louie now had serious infections, I thanked God that when he arrived he had been placed in one of the private rooms. I could not imagine having to visit him while standing as close to his neighbor as to him. His room was quite small, but it did have a sink, a window, a cabinet, and a bulletin board. There was no chair, but I knew visits would be so short that I would not have time to sit anyway. With the ventilator in the room, there was just a little room to get on either side of the bed.

When I arrived at LifeCare that morning, I had to sit in the waiting room until 10:00. The security guard at the desk just outside the glassed-in waiting room motioned to me when it was time for me to go up to the second floor where the Observation Unit was located. When I finally got to see Louie, he was pretty groggy from the sedation given the night before. The nurses indicated that his vital signs were much better. It felt as if we were starting over. I knew he would have to stay in this intensive care unit for days due to the infection, and that would mean I would be commuting to Rocky Mount each day.

I asked Louie's nurse as many questions as I could think of about his condition. I did not see a doctor that day. One cannot imagine how apprehensive I now felt because of the turn of events. I was asking myself over and over if I had made the right choice by bringing him to LifeCare. However, I would pray between visits, and God would reassure me that all things were in His hands.

95

The waiting room was quite small with only about a dozen straight chairs and a couple of tables. It was quite different from the large waiting room at Pitt Memorial. At Pitt the room had been bustling with visitors. The waiting room at LifeCare was not only small, but I believe I was the only person in that room all day. There was an overhead television in one corner by the door which was watched by the security guard across the hall. Although I had always rather enjoyed watching television at home when I didn't have anything else to do, I now found it to be rather annoying. I had absolutely no interest in watching television at the hospital nor when I was at home.

The security guard on duty during the weekdays apparently had a slight hearing problem, so the television was often loud enough to be intrusive to my thoughts and phone conversations. A few times in the days to come, I would request him to lower the volume. However, I realized he must have an extremely boring job just sitting there all day, so I tried to tolerate the noise since it was the guard's only diversion. The guard on weekends kept the volume quite low or turned it off, which was a relief.

Not only was the waiting room empty on that first day, I was to learn that this was the pattern for days to come. Very few visitors joined me there. With only five patients in the Observation Unit, there just weren't that many visitors waiting. Some of those other four patients were apparently from some distance away, and their family members obviously could not visit every day. Visitors coming to see patients who were not in the Observation Unit usually went directly to their rooms and did not have to stop by the waiting room. Occasionally a visitor would sit in the waiting room while the patient was having a bath or some medical procedure. There were a few more visitors usually on the weekends.

I quickly realized that this was going to be quite a different experience from the one I had at Pitt Memorial. I would not be surrounded each day by my friends nor would I have the pleasure of chatting very much with other patients' family members. I wondered what God's plan was for this new situation. I was sure He had a purpose, so I decided to try to stay open to whatever He had planned. This had already been such a faith-building experience so far, I knew God must be planning to use this new experience to teach me something.

On each of my visits with Louie that day, he seemed to be about the same. At the end of the day, I drove home for a night's rest. At six the next morning, I had a call from LifeCare. When I saw the name on caller ID, my heart sank again! "What now?" I thought. It was not bad news, thankfully. The nurse was calling to ask my permission to remove Louie's PICC line and to replace it with a central line because it was possible that the PICC line was the source of infection.

Although the PICC line had recently been inserted at Pitt Memorial because it could stay in longer—up to a year I was told—and had less chance of an infection than a central line, I had no choice but to give permission over the phone for the procedure.

When I arrived at the hospital later that morning, Louie was receiving physical therapy, for which I was very grateful. I knew those limbs had to be moved if he would ever recover his strength.

He was more alert on this occasion, and was very frustrated that I could not read his lips nor his writing (scribbling), though he seemed amazed that I couldn't understand him. Often his lips barely moved as he mouthed words to me. I knew he thought he was emphasizing words, but I just couldn't make them out. When he became upset, I also became upset. Often when he would scribble something, he would look at me expectantly as if wondering why I couldn't read it. Sometimes the scribbles were all in one spot on the paper, and other times it was just a wavy line or a line that would run off the page.

I would encourage him to point to letters on the alphabet sheet I had created, but he would not point to the alphabet letters one at a time to spell out words to me. I was not sure whether he could even comprehend the alphabet or was able to spell words. It really hurt my feelings when I could not understand him and knew how frustrating it was to him.

I longed to see him well enough to share what was going on inside his head. I also wanted to know that there was not permanent brain damage that prevented him from writing. Knowing what beautiful handwriting he had before his surgery, it was very hard to look at those squiggles he considered to be writing.

I still had to don a disposable gown and rubber gloves each time I visited him. This took precious minutes away from my already short time allowed for a visit. Sometimes it would take me the rest of my fifteen-minute visit to figure out something Louie was trying to share, only to learn that it was not something of earthshaking importance. One day after he had struggled to tell me something, he finally was able to write one very shaky word on his notepad. The word was "slant." I had no idea what "slant" meant to him! After many questions about the position of his bed and his body, I finally figured out that he wanted the wedge-shaped pillow in his room to put to his back. He couldn't think of "wedge," so he had written "slant." I placed the pillow to his back, but by then, my time was up, and I had to go.

As usually happened, when I would tell him I had to go, he would look so sad and disappointed that it would break my heart. He could not seem to grasp why I could only visit for fifteen minutes every two hours.

His brother Robert eventually brought him a couple of small white boards with erasable markers. As Louie improved, he was eventually able to print words on these boards that were more legible, and it was quite a relief when I found that what he wrote made sense.

During the time when he was still mouthing words to me, I could make out one recurring question from him. "Why am I here?" Each day for the first several days we were at LifeCare, I would explain that we were in Rocky Mount at LifeCare Hospital and that we were there to help him get weaned off the ventilator. I always reassured him that he was doing very well. I would tell him that as soon as he was off the ventilator, we would be going home or possibly to PCMH first for physical therapy.

Because I wasn't sure he understood where he was, I decided to make pictures of the hospital to show him. I included pictures of the outside of the hospital, the parking lot, the waiting room where I spent so much time, the cafeteria, and even the sign hanging in the waiting room that said "LifeCare Hospitals of North Carolina." Even though he never mentioned it, I wondered if he thought he might be in a nursing home. I wanted him to know that this was not going to be a permanent residence. I showed him the pictures several times, which I had printed on 8 ½ x 11-inch paper so he could see them clearly,

I did not tell him details about what he had experienced during his crisis. As he asked questions, I would give honest answers with minimum details. As he grew stronger, I shared a little more each time. I felt he needed to be stronger before having to deal with all that had happened to him.

Something else that I did during this time also involved the use of pictures. I posted a recent picture of our grandson, Jansen, on Louie's little bulletin board for him to enjoy, and I posted two photos of Louie himself on the board. One was a picture of Louie in his hospital gown at Pitt Memorial the day before his surgery. Dana had made the picture with her cell phone, and Louie looked very fit and very happy. At that time, Louie was sporting a beard and mustache he had grown for just a couple of months before the surgery. The other photo was another picture Dana had made of her dad outside a restaurant while we were waiting to be seated. It showed Louie in street clothes, sans the beard, a few months before he went into the hospital.

I did not post these pictures for Louie. I posted them for the nurses and other caretakers to see how good he looked before his health crisis. I wanted these photos to be an inspiration to them to get him back to the good health he had before surgery.

By this time, the antibiotics seemed to be helping his infection— whatever the infection was. He still had the C. diff. stomach bug that caused extreme diarrhea. His blood pressure and temperature were doing fine.

That evening, May 2, I updated my prayer partners by e-mail as was my nightly ritual. The last paragraphs of that message explained to them why I included so many details in my messages.

If you wonder why I give so many medical details, it is because these e-mails are also my journal of what has happened during this ordeal. I have printed these messages, and as of today I've started carrying them with me. The staff at LifeCare keep asking me questions about what happened at Pitt Memorial that was not included in the medical records. These notes have become very helpful for a reference. Just thought you might like to know why I include so many details—just killing two birds with one stone!

Thank you again and again for all your prayers!

Little did I realize at the time that this journal would be the beginning of a book.

Chapter 12

Trusting in God

The LORD is my rock, and my fortress, and my deliverer;
my God, my strength, in whom I will trust; my buckler, and
the horn of my salvation, and my high tower.
(Psalm 18:2) KJV

On Sunday, May 4, I sent the following e-mail in the morning before leaving home to visit Louie:

Louie was very sleepy yesterday. They had given him sedation about 8 p.m. Friday night, and it had not worn off. He would open his eyes, but was not very responsive. I thought he would be more alert as the day went on. Bud and Judy came to visit at 2 p.m., and he was about the same. When Dana came at 4 p.m. I thought he would be awake, but the nurse had given him Benadryl, and he was totally asleep. Dana had made the hour's drive for a 15-minute visit only to see him sleeping! I hated that he didn't get to see her. He needs the encouragement of seeing his family and friends. However, there was nothing I could do about it.

Louie's hemoglobin was down to 8, so they gave him 2 more units of blood yesterday. The nurses think he is lethargic because of his low blood count. I think it is primarily the meds, but then that is only the opinion of "Dr. Tyndall"! This sedation issue is really, really bothering me. I don't want Louie to be anxious and agitated to the extreme, but I worry that he is being overmedicated.

Since this was on my mind, I started to call his nurse several times during the night. Finally, at 4 a.m. I called and asked about him. His nurse said he was more alert. I expressed the desire to speak to his doctors, since I haven't actually had a conversation with anyone except the PA and that was when he first arrived and had not been evaluated yet. She said it would probably be Monday morning, and she would request that the PA talk to me.

It is so frustrating! Perhaps Monday morning I can finally capture a doctor to find out what the plan is for Louie.

Please keep praying for Louie's recovery, the doctors'/ nurses' wisdom and skill, and my patience!

Things were a little better when I visited Louie that same day. I wrote in another message when I got home

Louie was more alert today, but not quite as responsive as he was on Friday. One good thing is that the diuretic has caused him to lose at least 20 pounds of fluid! He had put on 50-60 pounds of fluid, so hopefully in a few days his body will get rid of all this excess.

He is running a slight fever, and we should have the results of all the cultures tomorrow. Hopefully then we will know what is causing his infection. He still has the stomach bug as far as I know, but he's on several antibiotics. Hope they take care of all his problems. Ironically, one of the causes of the stomach bug is excessive use of antibiotics! It's certainly a Catch 22!

I spoke to his pulmonary doctor, Dr. Boseman, this afternoon and liked her very much. She answered a bunch of questions for me and made me feel lots better about Louie's progress. She, too, had been very pleased with his responsiveness on Friday. Maybe tomorrow will be another good day.

After the two units of blood yesterday, Louie's hemoglobin was up from 8 to 10. The nurse said she would like to see it at 14.

We're still on the roller coaster. Some days are better than others. We realize there are still more hurdles ahead. Please pray that Louie can get off the ventilator before they have to move his feeding tube from his nose to his stomach. I shudder to think of another incision, especially since he has all that hernia repair with the mesh over most of his abdomen. Incisions are what caused most of his hernia problems, and I don't know exactly how they would deal with this if he has to have a feeding tube put in his stomach.

Pray that I can stay focused on God and His will in each situation. Sometimes my impatience tends to cause me to run ahead of God! Each day I need to submit all my concerns to Him because He is actually the only one in absolute control!

Thank you for your love and concern and prayers!

By Monday Louie was more alert. He had not been given sedation the night before nor during the day. He was a bit sleepy from not getting enough sleep the night before, but this was a more natural kind of sleepiness rather than a drug-induced sleep.

We were still waiting for the results of the cultures to know the cause of his infection. His temperature was 99, his white count was good, and his hemoglobin was still 10. They had not weighed him the previous day, but I noticed the swelling in his legs and arms was diminishing. I was anxious for them to begin the vent weaning — what we had come to LifeCare for in the first place. I realized, however, that with the sudden onset of the infections, his caregivers had to take care of more important things first.

One issue I had when I first saw Louie in his room at LifeCare was the length of his bed. Since Louie is 6 feet 4 inches tall, he never fits in a regular bed. I had to request a longer bed at Pitt Memorial, and I had also requested a longer bed at LifeCare. I had discussed the bed issue before he had been moved and had been assured that Louie would have a long bed when he arrived in Rocky Mount. It had not happened yet, and we had been there nearly a week. He was having to lie with his knees bent to prevent his feet from resting against the foot board. I did not want to be ugly to anyone, but I finally said to the nurse on duty, "This bed is just not acceptable. We were assured he would have a bed long enough before we came here; he has now been here a week, and we still do not have a satisfactory bed." The nurse assured me they were working on getting a longer bed. In the meantime, they tried to arrange his legs and pillows in such a way that he was halfway comfortable. The next day he finally got his longer bed.

I usually ate breakfast and lunch each day in the small cafeteria on the first floor. It was open for breakfast and lunch on Mondays through Fridays, and the food was much better than most institutional food. There were also drink and snack machines and a microwave oven available. Sometimes when I needed to get out of the waiting room, I would go to the cafeteria between mealtimes to write thank-you notes or to make phone calls or to get away from the television.

The hospital was located less than five minutes from a large shopping area with plenty of restaurants. Since I didn't like to shop, I opted to stay at the hospital all the time. I told my friends that as time went on and I grew more stir crazy, I might have to try out some of the nearby stores, and eventually I did. Also, on weekends when the hospital cafeteria was closed, I had to leave the hospital to get meals at nearby restaurants. Several times when friends visited they would take me to lunch or dinner at one of these restaurants.

One amazing thing that happened while I was spending all this time in Rocky Mount concerned my eating habits. I really needed to lose some weight, and before Louie became sick, I had just lost 10 pounds, intending to continue dieting and take off even more. Once he went into the hospital, I tried to eat nutritious food at least once a day. However, there were many times, both in Greenville and weekends in Rocky Mount, when it was necessary for me to partake of fast food. Since I hated eating alone, it was easier to get food at a drive-thru than to go inside a restaurant and sit alone. I figured I would gain lots of weight as a result of my poor diet and lack of exercise, but God even took care of that. I did not lose any weight, but I did not gain a pound during this time.

By now Louie's stomach bug seemed to be gone. He had begun having physical therapy five times a week, and I was very thankful for that. It didn't appear that they were able to do much about the vent weaning yet, but I was hoping they would start soon.

One week after Louie arrived at LifeCare, I found him sitting in a chair, having been hoisted from the bed, for the first time at my 12 noon visit. I knew he must have found this very exciting as well and also restful to his back to sit upright for a while. He was exhausted when I visited him later at 2:00, but I thought it was such an encouraging sign for him to be up.

A friend of ours who is a physician's assistant visited me at home one evening. He wanted to make certain that I understood what a long process Louie's recovery was going to be. He reminded me of the possibility of lots of other complications that could arise. I had already thought many times about those possibilities, but I had decided not to borrow trouble by focusing on those possibilities. I had decided to take one day at a time. I wanted to be realistic enough to know there could still be more possible bumps in the road along the way, but I was not going to expect them. We would just have to deal with them as they came. In the meantime, we would give thanks for the baby steps of progress we were making and deal with the setbacks as best we could, if and when they came.

I wrote to my friends that evening

> God has spared Louie for a purpose. I don't know what that purpose is, but God does! He can be trusted with Louie's life and his health. I must keep my eyes on Jesus. He is my Rock and my High Tower. He has promised not to leave nor forsake us. I know that He is faithful!
>
> Thank you for continuing to lift us up in prayer!

The next day did prove to be one of the bumps in the road. Louie had developed a severe rash. They thought at first it was a reaction to one of the several antibiotics he was on, so they changed his meds. Later they told me that it was a reaction to Lomotil, an over-the-counter medicine they were giving him to help his stomach. They had put him on Benadryl and a topical antibiotic cream to help the rash. By the next day he looked like a red lobster. His body from head to toe was like one gigantic blister. Thankfully, he did not seem to hurt nor itch from this rash, but it was scary looking. In a day or two it began to fade, but later his body would peel all over—even shedding the tough, calloused skin on the bottoms of his feet.

I was still concerned about his sedation meds. Part of my e-mail on May 8 expressed that concern.

I spoke to his pulmonary doctor (Dr. Boseman) today, and she answered many of my questions. Apparently, he simply cannot come off the sedative totally. They are giving it only when he doesn't sleep all night and becomes very agitated. This, too, will have to be a weaning process. Since I trust Dr. Boseman, I'm going to try to live with this plan.

Dr. Boseman said they had actually started reducing his ventilator support yesterday. It will be a little change each day, but it is a beginning.

Later in the afternoon I had a conference with his other caregivers—his nurse, respiratory care person, nutritionist, pharmacist, occupational and physical therapists, and several others. They plan to talk to his doctor about trying a smaller dose of sedative or either a different sedative. The sedative seems to zap him for 24 or more hours, and then communication is so difficult. I want him to have what he needs to be comfortable, but I hate having him zonked so much! I feel he would be less agitated if he could get to the point where he could communicate better.

We continue to take one day at a time—sometimes one hour at the time. God is good, and I know His grace is sufficient to get us through this!

Thank you for your love and concern and prayers!

These informational meetings I had mentioned, called "rounds" by the hospital staff, were provided every week for patients' families. The first one was a little intimidating since I didn't know what to expect. I was ushered into a conference room by Zeke, who was in charge of Respiratory Care. There, seated at a large conference table and in extra chairs around the room, were the people I mentioned in the e-mail—probably 12 or more people. I was seated in a side chair facing the group. Each person gave a report from his/her point of view regarding Louie's condition and care. At times they even provided photographs of his rash or other skin breakdowns.

I remember being asked at this first meeting something like this, "Mrs. Tyndall, what are your expectations regarding your husband when he is released from LifeCare?"

My emphatic response was, "I expect my husband to recover and be restored to the health level he had before this crisis. I expect to take him home—possibly by way of Pitt Memorial Rehab for a few weeks of physical therapy. However, if you can do sufficient physical therapy here to eliminate the need to go back to the hospital in Greenville for rehab, that would be just great."

No one commented on my outlook, and everyone tried not to show any doubt on their faces, but I felt in my spirit that there was a sense of skepticism in some minds that this would be a reality. I knew they realized they had their work cut out for them in view of Louie's serious condition. I also knew that God was going to be helping them every step of the way. I was praying for a miracle, and I completely believed God was going to give us one.

Once each one had given a report at the meeting, I had the opportunity to ask questions. You may have already surmised that I always had questions. That first day I had a notepad with me that contained an entire page of questions. I took that notepad with me every time I went to "rounds."

One of my questions on this day was the issue of diabetes. As I had discussed with nurses at Pitt Memorial and at LifeCare, I now mentioned to this group of staff members that Louie had not had diabetes before entering the hospital. Once again I was told that he may not have been tested properly before or he may have only been borderline before. He still had diabetes and needed the insulin. I expressed my hope that we would not go home with diabetes.

I found these meetings to be extremely helpful. Not only did they keep me informed, but they gave me an opportunity to voice my concerns and to ask questions about things I did not understand. I found everyone there to be extremely cooperative. As a result of my concern about the amount of sedation given, they decided to cut down on Louie's dosage when they learned how long he remained sleepy after they were administered.

Also, on any occasion when I asked for information, I received a prompt response. For example, once I requested a list of every medicine Louie was on and the purpose for each one, and I was brought a printed list by the pharmacist to the waiting room just a few minutes after the meeting was over. I truly felt that they listened to my concerns and kept me informed.

By now my confidence in the decision to move Louie to LifeCare was growing. Louie's brother Robert confirmed my decision and was certain I had done the best thing for Louie's well being.

Chapter 13

Blessings

I thank my God upon every remembrance of you.
(Philippians 1:3)

On Monday, May 12, I sent the following e-mail:

I have no major changes to report for Louie on Sunday
or today. His rash is clearing up—thankfully! His pulmonary
doctor says they are making small adjustments in his ventilator. It will be a trial and redo program and will be slow. The
doctor will not project how long it might take to get him off
the vent.

Getting off the vent is the major prayer need now. When
Louie can get off the vent, he will be able to talk and hopefully can begin to eat again. I'm also praying that we will
not have to go to a stomach feeding tube, as I've mentioned
before.

The days don't get any easier. It breaks my heart every
time I'm with Louie to see him so helpless. I just have to
continue to focus on God and remind Louie that God's grace
is sufficient to get us through this!

All of you have been so faithful with your prayers. My
prayer for you is that God will bless each one of you for your

awesome love and commitment and intercession! Louie and I are so blessed to have such a wonderful Christian family!

The next day brought another potential bump in the road. On Tuesday I wrote to my friends

Today was another decision-making occasion. When I arrived at LifeCare this morning, I learned that the doctor planned to insert a feeding tube in Louie's stomach tomorrow! I had to do some fast scrambling to get in touch with his original surgeon in Greenville, Dr. Pendleton, to get his input on this plan. He called me back just before 2:00 and said he preferred that the surgery he performed not be tampered with for 6 months, but at the very least 3 months, which would mean another 4 weeks before doing a stomach tube.

After discussing this with Dr. Pendleton, discussing it with other family members, and praying about it, I told the nurse I would not be signing a release to do the procedure. When I arrived home this afternoon, someone from LifeCare called regarding my decision. When I explained how extensive Louie's surgery was and the fact that the mesh covered his whole abdominal area, I finally convinced them that it was too risky to pierce this area with a tube. There are risks involved with keeping the feeding tube in his nose, but I had to weigh the risks and make the best decision I could. The lady calling from LifeCare agreed that I had made the right decision based on the information I shared with her. They will be requesting a copy of Dr. Pendleton's CT scan for future reference. Wouldn't it be wonderful if he could be weaned from the vent and eating normal food before we have to consider the stomach tube again?

The respiratory care person was with Louie on my last visit. He said they had turned down Louie's pressure on the vent today and that he had done very well with it. He turned it up again for the night but plans to turn it down again for a longer period of time tomorrow. This is how the weaning process works. That was good news to us!

Louie was very alert today and looked better than he has for several days. The rash is nearly gone.

Prayers are being answered! Keep praying!

It seemed another potential crisis had been avoided. I could not have imagined how distraught Louie would have been had a stomach tube been inserted that upset the original surgery that led to this crisis in the first place. With all that had happened, I definitely did not want anything to undo that hernia repair. It had been a physically costly procedure.

At my next "rounds" meeting, I was told that Louie was off antibiotics, his physical therapy was going well, the vent weaning was progressing slowly, the rash was gone, and his edema was improving. It was now time for a goal date to be set for his discharge. I was excited to hear that the date set was May 29, but I was quickly told that this date was set by someone in administration, not his doctor, and that it was not very realistic. The staff assured me that Louie's doctor would pay no attention to this goal date but would treat him cautiously as she saw fit.

I was encouraged nonetheless, and I was excited that Louie would have this potential discharge date posted in his room so that I could share with him that the end of his hospital stay was in sight. I did tell him that he would likely have to go back to Pitt Memorial for more rehab but that we were definitely making progress.

By May 17 Louie was looking much better. His edema was improving, and his arms and legs were beginning to look normal again. He was sitting up more each day after being hoisted from his bed, a procedure I could not watch. I had seen the device used to hoist him from bed, but I could not bear to watch my 6' 4" 250-pound husband dangling in the air between the bed and the chair. I love watching surgeries and other medical procedures on television, but for some reason this particular activity was unnerving to me.

I continued to tell Louie about how blessed we were to have so many wonderful friends who were lifting us up in prayer every day. I also told him how blessed he was that God had brought him so far. While I still did not go into any details at this point with him about all that had happened to him, I tried to answer his questions as briefly as I could without misleading him. I would reassure him that he was healed from the initial surgery. I let him know that there had been some complications from the procedure, but things were getting better.

As he realized on his own how seriously ill he had been, he became more and more emotional. When this happened, I told him that I was sure God had a purpose in all that had happened and that He obviously had something else very important either for Louie to do or to be!

I wrote in my daily message to friends and family that day

As Louie becomes more aware of what he has been through and how serious his condition has been (and still is), he is more emotional. We continue to struggle with communication, but sometimes I can read his lips, and sometimes I can read his notes. We muddle through!

According to Cliff, who visited him last night, Louie still has a bit of ICU psychosis. Louie shared a story with Cliff that was quite off the wall! The nurse says that this phenomenon is most common in the late afternoon/evening hours. Louie also told Dana and Michael this afternoon that he had seen his hospital bill, which he has not! This is not alarming but expected after all he's been through and how long he's been in ICU.

We continue to hang in there with Jesus—the only way to go!

Visitors in the next few days observed a great improvement in Louie. He was regaining some of his strength. I wrote to my friends that I knew he was getting stronger because I had arm wrestled him, and he was able to hold his own against me. I did point out that this was not saying a lot because he didn't have much competition.

On May 21 Louie was sitting in his special chair when I arrived and looked very bright-eyed. The respiratory therapist came in and told us he was turning off Louie's ventilator for the first time. I was overjoyed! They kept him off for an hour, and he did very well.

Later that afternoon, he was kept off for another hour. The plan was to increase the time off the ventilator a little each day.

He was also beginning to pull himself up just a little in bed using the trapeze bar hanging over his bed. The therapists also had him put some weight on his feet from the side of the bed, although he had not yet stood up. I was so thankful for every little improvement.

His feeding tube had to be replaced about this time, which was no picnic for him. The good news was that it was replaced with a smaller tube that could stay inserted longer without causing nasal problems. This had been a concern since we learned a stomach feeding tube was not feasible.

On May 23 I wrote to everyone

Louie was very sleepy this morning at my first visit. I think the physical therapist had given him a real workout. There was a walker in the room. I asked Louie if he had been able to stand, and he said no. However, later his nurse said he did stand, so I don't know who was right. Guess I'll have to wait until I talk to the therapist again. He was soundly sleeping at my last two visits!

He continues the weaning process on the respirator—two hours off each day. Hope next week he can get off much longer each day.

When our friend Cliff Cahoon visited him this afternoon, Louie had lots of questions about the garden. He and Cliff had started the garden together, but Cliff has been left with all the work! Last week Cliff took Louie a bunch of 8 1/2 x 11 photos of the garden including the peach trees. Louie asks me to show the photos to everyone who visits!

I took the CD player today, and Louie was listening to Sandi Patti when I left him. He has a TV in the room, but he doesn't seem very interested in it.

No other news about Louie, but I did hear from my cousin Jesse [who is like my brother] this afternoon. The scan shows his pancreas has a mass about 1/2-inch square, and they suspect it is cancer. However, it does not appear to have spread. He will be in touch with his cardiologist next week in preparation for surgery. Please keep him in your prayers along with Louie. As I told Jesse, this problem was found by "accident" while doctors were doing a routine check of his aneurysm repair. I believe that God had the doctors find it early so that it could be treated before it spread. We continue to trust in God and give Him this problem as well.

There are so many people with problems at LifeCare. I speak to some of their loved ones in the waiting room. One lady who is visiting her husband there has herself had breast cancer, ovarian cancer, and recently lung cancer. She had just completed her chemotherapy this last time when her husband had to go to LifeCare. With all this, her attitude is one of trust in God and obvious peace in the midst of this storm.

Another lady I spoke to is there for her mother. Yesterday, she told me they were moving her mother to Nash General Hospital to amputate her foot! She was back at LifeCare today! The daughter was doing remarkably well in view of this crisis and said her mom was also doing well!

I could go on and on with stories like this. I don't mean to sound depressing. On the contrary, each day I realize there are so many people who have more problems than I do. I am also very touched by the faith of these family members as they trust their loved ones to a wonderful Lord!

So far I haven't met anyone whose problems I would swap for my own!

Please remember all those at LifeCare and other hospitals who have such dire needs.

Thank you for all your prayers and messages of love and concern!

The next day Louie was able to be off the ventilator for two hours in the morning and two hours in the afternoon. I was finally able to begin reading him some of the many get-well cards he had received. This was very emotional for him but in a very good way.

In the afternoon Dana had a nice visit with her dad while I kept Jansen in the lobby. What a joy to his Nana's heart to spend some time with my little sweetheart.

By May 26 Louie was off the ventilator three hours in the morning and three hours in the afternoon. I felt he had really turned a corner and was making more rapid progress. To him I'm sure the progress seemed quite slow, but at least it was progress rather than a step backward.

The only thing Louie ever mentioned that he wanted was a few drops of water. His mouth was always so dry. We tried to keep it moistened with swabs, but it just was not the same as a drink of water.

May 27 was a momentous day. My e-mail for that day says it all.

Good news! When I walked in this morning for my 10:00 visit, Louie greeted me by SAYING, "I love you." That's right, he SAID it! The speech therapists were with him, and they had just set the valve on the trach so that he could talk. They left it that way for the 15-minute visit. Pastor Grant Carter was there with me to witness Louie's first words in a long time! They did the same procedure for my 4:00 visit, and he got to talk again. How good to hear his voice!

Also, he stood for the first time today during physical therapy. It may have been only for a second, but he stood! The therapists were very pleased. So am I!

He's been off the vent 3 hours in the morning and 3 hours in the afternoon. Tomorrow, they will try keeping him off 6 continuous hours! Yay!

Friends Glenn and Mac Swanson were there for the 12:00 and 2:00 visits. They think Louie looks great. Louie said the nurses told him he has lost 49 pounds of fluid since he's been at LifeCare! He hardly recognizes his own feet and hands—they're so small compared to what they were a few weeks ago!

I share with him every visit how many people are praying for him, and he is so grateful for each of you and every prayer!

I told him that when he is well, if we never do anything the rest of our lives but praise the Lord for his mercy and grace and give thanks for our friends, it would not be enough!

Thank you, thank you, thank you again for each prayer! We are so blessed with loving family and friends!

The next day, May 28, was another milestone. Here's what I wrote on that day.

Louie was kept very busy this morning. When I arrived for the 10:00 visit, he was off the vent, had just had physical therapy, and was working with the occupational therapists. They had him stand up briefly as they assisted him in getting into his chair. They rolled his chair to his doorway so that he had a different view for a while as he practiced pedaling with his hands.

As soon as the OT was finished, his speech therapists arrived. They worked with him on talking and swallowing. Joyful day, he was allowed to suck the moisture off a plastic spoon that had been dipped in ice chips and water! His eyes lighted up as if it were Christmas at the prospect of having a few drops of water! Then they actually let him have a few ice chips to practice swallowing! That's the only thing he has ever asked for—some water! He's been waiting 10 weeks, so he loved it! He did very well with his swallowing on this first trial.

The [local] pastor who comes every Wednesday was entertaining ambulatory patients in the hallway by playing and singing hymns outside the Observation Unit during all this therapy time. When the pastor finished, he came into the Unit, parked his keyboard in front of Louie, and sang "How Great Thou Art." We both cried!

I ended up staying in the Unit with Louie nearly an hour and a half since I was not actually talking to him but observing his therapy. The nurse was very kind to let me do this! I only had to wait half an hour before my next visit! This was unusual, but a nice treat.

Louie stayed off the vent 6 straight hours today. He was tired when I left, but we are both so pleased that he's doing well and is up to all this therapy. It surely was busy all around him today. The nurses and other caregivers all seem to love Louie, and he returns their affection. His pulmonary doctor visited while I was with him. She thinks he is doing well. She is going to be on vacation for a few days but has promised to call and check on him every day.

Thank God for calling people to minister to the sick. They have very tough jobs—jobs I could not begin to do.

On a sad note, please pray for two ladies I met at LifeCare, Brenda and Jean, who lost their mother yesterday. There were about a dozen family members visiting on Monday who knew the end was near. Thankfully, these two ladies are Christians, as was their mother; however, losing a loved one is never easy. I know God's peace will get them through. **Phil. 1:3**

Chapter 14

Great Is Thy Faithfulness

. . .His compassions fail not. They are new every morning:
great is Thy faithfulness. (Lamentations 3:22-23) KJV

A s I continued to travel each day to Rocky Mount, I calculated that I had driven nearly 4500 miles while he was in LifeCare. Since I was not having a quiet time at home, I used the time on the road each morning to pray and to praise God for His mercy and grace. Each day as I made that trip of about 55 miles, I thanked Him that it was spring, and the weather was good. Had this crisis occurred in winter, I might have had to worry about icy roads. However, the days were always bright and sunny, helping my outlook on life tremendously.

Part of the trip was on a secondary road where there was little traffic, which allowed me to concentrate on my prayers more freely. I sometimes had my radio on a Christian station or had one of my Christian CDs playing, and there were many times when a particular song or sermon spoke directly to my need for that day. Usually by the time I arrived in Rocky Mount, my heart was singing for the joy of the Lord! God was always blessing me in so many ways.

God was also blessing Louie. On Friday, May 30, I wrote the following to my praying friends:

Louie was off the vent for 7 hours today. He continues with his physical therapy, occupational therapy, and speech therapy. He loves the speech therapist because she comes bearing ice chips!

He had lots of company today. Pastor Grant Carter was there for the 10:00 visit, Bud and Judy McLawhon and Norman and Linda Brooks were there for the 12:00 visit, and his nephew Carl and wife Barbara were there at 2:00. He enjoyed each visitor and was able to talk to all of them!

Dr. Mendez from PCMH (Pitt County Memorial Hospital) has been checking on Louie. She is following his progress so that she can do a referral for him to have therapy at the Rehab Center when he is off the vent. He will have to be totally off for a few days before he can move back to Pitt. We do hope this will be soon, but no one has given us a projected date yet.

Louie's weight is back to his pre-surgery level. Apparently, he is finally rid of all the excess fluid. He is feeling very thin! He hardly recognizes his feet and legs and hands after all the edema he had for so long. His legs are actually smaller than he has seen them in some time because he had some swelling in them before going to the hospital.

We are so blessed by God's grace and mercy in bringing Louie to this point in his recovery, and we are so blessed to have each of you who have supported us during this trial with your love and prayers!

Please remember my cousin, Jesse, in the coming week. He is scheduled to have surgery Monday, June 9, to remove the growth from his pancreas. I know God will walk with him through this ordeal and give him strength and comfort!

Also, please pray for the family of my friend, Mac Swanson, whose 19-year-old great nephew was killed in a motorcycle accident Thursday in Roanoke Rapids. Such a tragic loss!

Saturday things continued about the same, but Sunday was another red letter day. In the afternoon, Louie was moved out of the

Observation Unit into his own room. He had been at LifeCare four weeks and was finally well enough to get out of the ICU. This meant I could stay with him all the time. Even though this was unexpected, I was prepared to stay overnight. I had been hauling my bag in the trunk of my car since Louie first entered the hospital. It contained clothes and makeup and all the things I needed for a few nights' stay with him. I was ready to move in.

Since there was no Internet access at the hospital, I was not able to let all my friends know what was happening until Tuesday when I did make the trip back to Ayden to get fresh clothes and catch up on a few tasks at home. While I was at home that day, I sent the following message to our friends:

Good news! Louie was moved out of the ICU unit into his own room Sunday afternoon! Yay! It's so good to have more space and more privacy and to know that he's well enough to be in his own room.

Since this was not completely anticipated, I didn't have a chance to let all my prayer partners know. Hope none of you were worried about not getting a message. I spent Sunday night in the room with Louie and last night as well. Thankfully, I had been hauling some extra clothes and other items just in case he got moved and I got to stay with him. I came home just now to get fresh clothes, pay bills, answer phone calls, and e-mail you guys! I'll be heading back shortly, so if you don't hear from me, it will be because I'm without computer access at the hospital.

Louie is staying off the vent about 10 hours at the time. He kept his speaking valve in all day yesterday. We had dear friends, Bruton and Frances Taylor, visit yesterday. They live in Roanoke, VA, and we don't see them often. I was so glad Louie could talk to them. Bruton was in college with Louie, and both of them were in our wedding.

Also, I surprised Eric yesterday by calling him in Minnesota and telling him someone wanted to speak to him. I think he was completely surprised when I put his Daddy on the phone for a real conversation. Both of them were pretty overwhelmed at the opportunity! What a blessing for me too!

I don't know how long it will be before Louie is given a swallow test. That will probably be the next big hurdle. Hopefully, when he passes the swallow test, they will be able to remove the feeding tube. That's the single most annoying thing happening to him at the hospital! He told our friends yesterday that he does not have any pain, which is another blessing, but the tube through his nose is uncomfortable.

As always I am so thankful for each little improvement, and I am so thankful for each of you—for your prayers, your love, your concern, your calls, your visits, your cards, your e-mails. You cannot imagine how much you have blessed us through this difficult time. I tell Louie all the time how wonderful our family and friends are! Along with our Lord, you have kept us going!

Love to each of you!

"His compassions fail not. They are new every morning: great is Thy faithfulness." (Lam. 3:22-23 KJV)

The first few nights I spent in the room with Louie were typical of nights I had spent with him on previous hospital stays. He did not sleep well at all, and neither did I. The staff had brought me a small cot to sleep on, but I never used it. I chose instead to sleep in my clothes in the recliner that was in the room, even though I had packed night clothes. There was a good reason why I made this choice.

For some reason Louie was very warm and needed the air conditioner set on about 60 degrees. Even though I have always been the one who was too warm and he was always cold natured, he now needed a very cool room. It was like a refrigerator in his room, and since he was the patient and seemed to be able to breathe better with the air cool, I decided to let him call the shots on temperature. I would have frozen to death on that cot, which was placed directly in the airflow from the air conditioner. I needed to sleep in my clothes nestled in my chair and covered by a blanket in order to stay warm— not that either of us slept very much those first few days.

I'm sure that being in a new location was difficult for Louie. Besides that, he still did not have his days and nights completely straight. During the night, as with all hospitals, caregivers were in and out of the room checking on him. In addition, the pulse oximeter on his finger would set off an alarm if he moved his hand, especially if he grasped the trapeze above his bed to try to turn or move in the bed. We could usually get the beeping to stop if I would remind him to hold his finger still for a few moments, but by then I would be wide awake. If we didn't get it to stop in time, the nurse would call over the speaker system to ask if everything was all right.

By the time morning arrived, I was very excited to get up and get a shower to wake up and to thaw out. I tried to do this early, around 6 a.m., before the nurses and aides came en masse and before the doctors made their visits.

Those first few days were very busy because Louie needed a lot of attention. His caregivers were very helpful and always came when they were needed, but since I was available, I tried to help as much as I could. Louie could not turn himself in bed. Not only did he not have the strength, he still had a hose attached to the ventilator, a feeding tube in his nose, a Foley catheter, a rectal tube, heart monitor with lines connected to leads all over his chest, and the pulse oximeter on his finger. When he moved, someone usually had to make sure that no lines were pulled loose.

He enjoyed having his back rubbed. Also, he had now begun to shed skin all over his body from the rash that had covered him. He peeled all over, but the strangest part was the tough, calloused skin on the bottom of his feet that also peeled. His feet looked extremely ragged all the time because that tough skin could not be pulled off. Our friend, Frances Taylor, who is a retired nurse, suggested I rub his feet with extra virgin olive oil. While there were several creams available that the caregivers often used, I rubbed his feet every day with the olive oil. I warned the staff that if his room smelled like an Italian restaurant, not to fear. It was only the olive oil.

Things began to move much faster once Louie was out of ICU and in his own room. I'm sure he did not think they were moving that fast, but I could see improvement each day. There were still some ups and downs, but primarily we were making progress.

We were looking forward to having Louie pass a swallow test so that he could begin eating and eventually get rid of the feeding tube. He did not pass the first one. Since I was only coming home twice a week at this time, my e-mails were much less frequent. However, by Friday, June 6, I was able to update my friends on my quick trip home:

Louie had his swallow test Wednesday and did not pass it. He didn't do the worst nor the best, according to his speech therapist. The doctor and his speech therapist assured us this is quite common not to pass the test the first try. He can be tested again in two weeks. We were a little discouraged at the news but tried to focus on the positive steps he is making.

Louie stayed off the vent 13 hours yesterday. They add an hour each day, and the respiratory therapist has predicted that he may be completely off the vent by the first or middle of next week! Great news!

Also, Louie walked several steps yesterday from his bed to the wall! He was quite pleased with this progress and so was I! He is now able to turn himself over in the bed too.

On the negative side, he does have a urinary tract infection, but they have started him on antibiotic, so we hope this will nip it in the bud soon.

While we still have a long way to go, we are so thankful for each improvement. The physician's assistant told Louie yesterday that when Louie came to LifeCare, he wasn't sure he would make it! Later when Dr. Boseman, his pulmonary doctor, came in, she told Louie that all his many friends' (and in many cases, strangers') prayers had made the difference!!!! Amen! We already knew that, but I was pleased to hear his doctor concur that God and the love and prayers of friends have brought about a miracle!

Besides each of you, there must be hundreds of others in the various churches you attend who are praying. I have encountered a bunch of strangers myself who have put Louie on their church prayer lists. We'll never know how many people have lifted us up in prayer! God is so good! I've never appreciated my faithful, committed Christian friends so much. My heart nearly bursts with the love I feel for you and for my faithful Lord and Savior and the gratitude I have for His mercy and grace!

Thank you, thank you, thank you for your prayers!

As Louie continued to improve and was able to walk a little, I was very encouraged. Although I thought Louie's attitude remained wonderful during most of this trial, he had a few moments occasionally when he felt a little discouraged. One day when I was so excited that he had walked a few steps, he commented that he didn't have the energy to go very far. "Listen," I said, "you're doing great. I remember when you couldn't even open your eyes! Be thankful for every little step."

He realized how true this was and agreed. Every time thereafter when he seemed a little disappointed that he couldn't do more, I would remind him of where he had been and how much progress he had made. Day by day it did not seem like major steps, but they were steps in the right direction. We had to measure progress by weeks to appreciate the results, not by days.

On Tuesday, June 10, I shared with friends this message:

Louie has been doing very well. When I returned to the hospital last Friday, I learned that he had walked from his bed to the hall and back. Yesterday (Monday) he walked down the hall past the nurses' station and back to his room! He had some assistance, of course, but I thought he did great!

He stayed off the vent 17 hours Sunday, and last night they adjusted the vent to only supply pressure, whatever that means! All I know is that it is another sign that he is soon going to be off the vent! I feel that we are right on the verge of coming off the vent, removing the feeding tube, and losing the catheter and rectal tube. There is light at the end of this dark tunnel!

Yesterday his speech therapist fed him some of Louie's own peaches from his prize peach tree. She had very kindly pureed them so he could at least sample some of the last ones from the tree. The speech therapist only allows him to eat snacks when she is with him giving him swallowing exercises. He is not quite ready to eat regular meals without her supervision. We'll be so glad when the NG (feeding) tube can be removed. It came out twice in one day and had to be reinserted, which is not fun for Louie! Hopefully, this time it will stay in place until it can be removed permanently.

This has been such an amazing journey. While it has been a very painful, difficult experience, I continue to see God's hand at work. I cannot begin to express how much my faith has grown during this ordeal. My love and appreciation for God has never been greater. Isn't it interesting how trials draw us closer to Him? In spite of the fact that Louie is the one who has done the suffering, he, too, has been able to see good things that have come from this trial. Romans 8:28 has proven to be true every day! I know for certain that my life and Louie's will never be the same after going through this crisis!

Please continue to pray for my cousin, Jesse. He had surgery yesterday, and the doctors removed 75 percent of his pancreas, which was malignant. While we were sorry to hear that news, we are praying for a full recovery. As evidenced by Louie's progress, we know God is still in the miracle-working business!

Thanks be to God for His wonderful love!

In the coming days Louie was able to walk longer distances with his physical therapist at his side, and sometimes another therapist would push his wheeled recliner chair behind him in case he became too tired to finish his walk. The hospital floor we were on was rectangular in shape with the nurses' station in the middle of the floor. Louie was able to walk around half the floor with assistance.

His occupational therapist was working with Louie on doing some things for himself such as dressing himself in his own pajamas and putting his shoes on. On one particular day after he had donned his own pajamas and shoes, he went for his regular walk around the floor. One therapist was beside him, and another therapist and I followed behind him. He had just passed the nurses' station and was moving down the hall, when his pajama bottoms fell completely off!

The therapist walking with me took a quick look behind us and assured him that none of the nurses at the station were looking, while the other therapist assisted him in getting his pants up. I nearly roared with laughter the rest of the way back to his room. It was a good feeling to be able to laugh at anything after such a long time in crisis mode.

By June 14 there was more positive news to share with my friends.

.

Well things are looking up for Louie! He walks each weekday around half the hospital floor, about 225 feet. Thursday he got rid of the urinary catheter, and yesterday they removed the rectal tube. Tomorrow night he will try going all night without the ventilator. Hopefully by Wednesday he will be off the vent! Yay!

Monday Louie has another swallow test. Please pray that he does very well on this. It will mean he can begin eating regular food and soon get rid of the feeding tube. At the moment, they are training me to feed him using the NG feeding tube just in case he has to come home with it. We're hoping that he will NOT have to come home with the feeding tube!

The rehab doctor from Pitt Memorial has determined that Louie is too good to go to rehab. Isn't that a wonderful problem! That means he will be coming straight home. He'll need some home health care for a while, but we can deal with that.

No one has given us a date, but based on the way things are moving, I'm hoping that we can come home in a couple of weeks.

It has been a long journey, and although it is not over yet, we do see light at the end of the tunnel. Please keep praying for a few more weeks!

We love you guys!

More good news was shared on Wednesday, June 18:

Well, Monday was a Red Letter day for Louie! First of all, he was off the vent all night Sunday and did very well. Monday morning he had his swallow test and did well on that. He was then permitted to have real food for lunch! He didn't think it tasted all that great, but we were very thankful for the progress. He can eat most foods, preferably in the soft category — no steak yet! He has to take two small bites and then drink "thickened" fruit drinks or tea or coffee. I can't tell you how yucky that stuff looks, and Louie says it is awful. Yesterday I bought him some tomato juice and V8 juice, which are permitted. I think they will be tastier! He can sip on water between meals. You remember, of course, he has been waiting for water for three months!

Monday his feeding tube had begun slipping out, so it had to be removed. I dreaded that it might have to be replaced, but God was good! The doctor agreed to let it stay out! Hallelujah! No more tube feedings!

Yesterday, Tuesday, the occupational therapist required Louie to give himself a bath. He continues to walk very well, usually around half the hospital floor. He is still not able to get up totally alone, but once he is assisted up, he can motor along pretty well with his walker.

Yesterday they also removed the ventilator from the room! Another praise! He continues to get a little oxygen, but they will soon wean him from that as well.

No one has given us a projected date for his coming home, but we hope it will be soon. I have a "rounds" meeting with all his caregivers at 2:00 today. Perhaps I'll learn more then.

My heart is so full of gratitude for God's grace and mercy in restoring Louie's health that it is nearly bursting with joy! We both continue to marvel at the love we have received from each of you and the excellent, loving care he has received at LifeCare. Their name is certainly appropriate!

I wish I had enough time to share with you all the wonderful, good things that have come out of this trying time. Only God can turn a bad thing into a blessing! Perhaps when Louie is home, I'll have time to share more about what God has done in our lives these past few months.

Thank you for your continued prayers. Please keep my cousin Jesse in your prayers as well. He's still in the hospital, but we're hoping he can come home soon.

We love you!

By Monday, June 23, we could finally see that a discharge from the hospital was in sight. We could hardly contain ourselves, but we also held our breaths that there would not be a complication to delay us.

June 23 I wrote the following:

As you recall, I have only been coming home from Rocky Mount about twice a week. I'm praying that this will be my last trip home alone! We are hoping that the next time I come home, Louie will be with me! Isn't that great news!

Louie has continued to do well with his weaning from the ventilator. He has only been getting a little bit of extra air in his trach at nights. I thought they would be removing the trach during the weekend or today at the latest, but Dr. Boseman forgot to write an order for him to be capped off all night last night, so we have to do that tonight. She said that this would not delay our departure.

Louie's blood pressure has been up a bit the last few days, so they've added extra meds for that. Hope that will not create a glitch in his progress. Please pray that all will continue to go well so that we can come home. He also continues to have a urinary tract infection, so they've started another round of antibiotics for that. Other than these two minor setbacks, he should be ready to come home soon.

Louie is gaining strength and improving in his ability to walk. He still struggles a bit to get up from a sitting position, but I can tell that this is also improving. He's able to give himself a bath and do lots more moving about in bed, so we know he's getting better.

Before we come home, I have to learn to test his blood sugar to keep his diabetes in check. He's currently getting insulin shots for this, so I may have to give shots also unless they change him to an oral medicine. He didn't have diabetes until he went into ICU at Pitt Memorial, so I'm praying that when he is better, he will recover from the diabetes. They tell me it is possible, however, I gather the staff doesn't think this is likely. However, you know I have no hesitation in praying that God will add this little need to His existing miracle!

Louie is eating regular foods but doesn't have much appetite. He fills up very quickly since his stomach was not accustomed to real food for so long. I'm sure the appetite will gradually come back. He is still supposed to drink thickened drinks, but they are so disgusting that he only drinks tomato juice with his meals. I can't blame him a bit. He has another swallow test this morning. If he passes this one, he can have regular liquids with his meals. I wanted to be there with him when he did the test, but I had a plumbing problem at home and needed to come in time to greet the plumber, who, incidentally, is here right now. Last week it was the air conditioner. Yet another challenge to our patience! We're really just grateful that both repairmen were able to respond so quickly when called.

When we get home, I will e-mail you and update you again. Hope that will be very soon.

Each time Louie and I have talked about the outpouring of love and prayers we have received from you guys, we cry together. God has certainly blessed us with the best friends and family in the world. We will always remember your many kindnesses to us!

God bless each of you!

Louie passed the swallow test that Monday, and he could then eat and drink anything he chose. On Tuesday they removed his trach. Things were really moving at warp speed now. We learned that Louie could go home on Thursday, June 26. Hallelujah! We were so elated.

On Wednesday Louie was taking his walk around the floor with his therapist, and I was tagging along with them. Zeke from Respiratory, who was always present at the rounds meetings, came up beside me and watched Louie as he made his way down the hall. Zeke said to me, "Do you remember what you told the staff at that first rounds meeting you attended about your expectations for Louie?"

"I certainly do," I replied. "I told you when asked what my expectations were for my husband that I expected him to get well and to return home in at least as good health as before his crisis, possibly making a detour to Pitt Memorial for more rehab. If LifeCare could give him enough physical therapy to bypass Pitt Memorial, that would be just great."

"That's right," Zeke remembered.

"I got what I asked for, didn't I?" I exclaimed.

I was so thankful that God had heard my prayers and the prayers of so many others and had granted our requests. The thought that "we have not because we ask not" crossed my mind, and I knew that it is so true. We must constantly ask God to meet our needs, even when by man's measure the odds seem impossible.

Because things were progressing so rapidly now at the hospital, we were beginning to get a wee bit anxious. We didn't talk about it, but I am sure both of us were wondering if we would be able to manage once we got home. Louie had been hooked up to so many devices for so long, what would it be like when there was nothing monitoring him? Would I be able to physically assist him in getting up and down? Would he have any sort of respiratory crisis?

As each of these fears crossed my mind, I would remind myself that God had been with us every step of the way. He was not going to forsake us now, but He would make a way to meet all our needs.

I marveled at how He had kept me so healthy during this entire time. I had not experienced any sickness or allergies or other problems while I was staying with Louie each day except for one brief scare. Two years before Louie's crisis I had experienced a ruptured disk that caused excruciating pain. I had to be transported by ambulance to Pitt Memorial hospital. While they did not diagnose the problem, later tests showed one ruptured disk and another bulging one. It took about a year and a half for my back to stop hurting every day. The disk that was bulging occasionally flared up and caused pain. When it did, I would take over-the-counter pain medicine and take it easy for a few days, and it generally would get better.

While we were at LifeCare and Louie was still in the Observation Unit, I had a day when out of the blue while I was in the waiting room, I felt that old familiar pain in my back. "Oh, no," I thought, "Not now. This is not a good time for me to have a problem! Lord, help me. I have to be here for Louie. What will I do if I can't get up and down to help him?"

As soon as I experienced the pain, I headed for the cafeteria to find a soft drink and to take a pain pill. It was lunch time when I opened the door to the cafeteria, and just as the door opened, a sharp pain went through my back that nearly caused my knees to buckle. Fortunately, I was holding on to the door, so I was okay, but I heard an audible gasp from several of the medical staff who had looked up just as I was about to enter the room. They apparently saw the pain on my face and saw me nearly crumble.

Right away they were so attentive and concerned, offering to help me. I just needed to sit down. Several people offered to get my lunch, but I had already eaten earlier. One kind young man offered his assistance, and I let him get my drink from the machine because I wasn't sure I could walk another step.

I took my pain pill and sat there for a while wondering what I would do if I were not able to walk back to the waiting room, much less drive home. Then I just had to turn it over to Jesus. He is my Strength and my Provider. He knew that I was there to minister to my husband. My prayer for healing was not a selfish prayer. I needed to be well so that I could do for Louie whatever I needed to.

In about half an hour, I decided to see if I could stand up. The cafeteria had pretty much cleared by now. I stood up carefully, and everything seemed to be okay. I walked slowly back to the waiting room, and I walked slowly and moved cautiously the rest of the day, but the pain did not return. Praise the Lord!

Other than that episode, I stayed quite well the many weeks we were in the hospital. My typical spring allergies did not even give me the usual problems. This was yet another of the many prayers that God was answering.

So many friends had offered us their assistance. Our friend Cliff was taking care of the garden he and Louie had started together. Now Cliff was left with all the harvesting to do, but he was doing an excellent job. His wife Cathy even took time from her busy schedule to water the houseplants and outside potted plants.

Everyone knew how fanatical Louie was over his yard, always keeping it manicured perfectly. Our friend Michael and our daughter Dana kept the yard in A-1 shape while we were in the hospital.

So many others offered to do things for us, but I really couldn't think of any other needs. The yard, garden, and plants were the only things that seemed to need attention. With my being gone all the time, I didn't have any needs at home. My Sunday School class kept asking what they could do for us, and I couldn't think of anything except to keep praying.

During that time when I was commuting daily to Rocky Mount, gas prices were at an all time high—nearly $4 a gallon. Like a lot of other things I had to put on the back burner, I did not spend much time worrying about how much gas I was using. However, others did. Both my Sunday School class and another Sunday School class at my church gave us very generous gifts of cash to apply toward our gas needs. What a blessing! The gifts were so generous, they paid for nearly my entire travel expenses going to and from Rocky Mount.

There were other thoughtful gifts as well, and hundreds of cards both to Louie and me. They were such an encouragement, and we would read those cards over and over. There was the blessing of the visits, of course, of family and friends. Louie's brother and sister-in-law came often from New Bern. Not only that, I was particularly grateful to his sister-in-law Debra, who has a beautiful singing voice, who came to Louie's bedside twice in Pitt Memorial while he was in ICU and sang without music. I'll never forget that first time she sang his favorite song, "How Great Thou Art." What a blessing! Later, at LifeCare she brought her guitar and entertained him in his room.

Once again I thanked God for His provision and for the wonderful blessing of having such loving family and friends.

We had grown quite close to many of the caregivers at LifeCare, especially those assigned to Louie most frequently. I hesitate to mention names since we were blessed by so many, but we had a special place in our hearts for one of his nurses, Pat, who took such good care of him in ICU and later, as well, when we were in a room. Also, our favorite CNA (Certified Nursing Assistant), Linda, was always so helpful and so kind to Louie. She really went beyond the call of duty many times to meet Louie's needs, and she remains very special in our hearts. It was people like these two caring ladies who made our upcoming departure a little tinged with sadness.

Surely enough, June 26 finally arrived, and Louie was going home. It was another busy day as we were saying farewells to staff members who seemed to linger in our room longer than usual, both of us hating to say goodbye. Besides that, the final devices were being removed from Louie one by one. The central line was removed, the heart monitor disconnected, and finally the pulse oximeter on his finger was removed. Louie said when the last item was removed, "I feel like Martin Luther King—free at last!"

I had been looking forward to driving Louie home when we left the hospital, but after some consideration we had decided to let him travel home by ambulance, figuring we might need some help to get him inside. The rest of our morning was spent waiting for the EMS team to arrive to transport Louie home. I believe we were both holding our breaths, fearful that some unknown setback would delay the discharge.

Just before we left, the nutritionist brought wonderful news. She said that Louie's blood sugar looked good, and he had not had insulin in three days. She recommended that we come home and continue to monitor his sugar level, but there was to be no insulin. Praise God! Another prayer had been answered.

The EMS team finally arrived. They whisked him onto the gurney and were on their way. As they took him to the ambulance entrance, I headed to the front door. I needed to arrive home a few minutes ahead of them to open the door, so I left just moments before his ambulance departed.

I made that last drive to Ayden with a light heart. I had only been home a few minutes when the ambulance arrived. The EMS team was having trouble getting the stretcher up the steps, so Louie offered to get off and walk up the steps if they would support him on both sides. He did just that. I met Louie at the door with the walker, and he actually walked to his recliner with assistance and sat down. We were finally home!

Louie said after he got in the house that the house looked strange to him. I said, "Well, it's probably because you came in the front door, which you're not accustomed to doing."

"No," he said. "My first thought on entering the house is that this is not my house. This is the most beautiful house I've ever seen." I presume it was his joy at being home that caused him to view his home in a new light.

After we got home and got settled, it was after midnight before I had time to let everyone know that we were home. It was a message too important to delay any longer, so I wrote the following message to my friends:

WE ARE HOME!

Can you believe that we're finally home? After 3 1/2 months—102 days in the hospital, to be exact—we are actually home! I'm pretty tired tonight after our exciting day, but I couldn't wait any longer to let you guys know the good news!

It has been a whirlwind week. Monday Louie passed his swallow test and was allowed to eat anything he wanted. That night, he went through the entire night with his trach capped. We thought he would have to do that two nights in a row, but on Tuesday morning, his doctor visited and said the trach could come out! The respiratory therapists were waiting in the hall that very minute to remove the trach. The doctor finally told us we could come home Thursday if nothing else changed. We have been counting the hours and minutes since then!

Louie did just fine with the trach removed—no problems at all. He could even speak clearly without holding his finger over the opening, which is covered with a piece of gauze and a bandage.

Wednesday was a very emotional day for both of us. I don't know why everything hit both of us at the same time, but I had come to realize I was going to miss my LifeCare family when we left! It may sound crazy as much as I wanted to come home, but those wonderful caregivers who, with God's help and the skill He has given them, have saved Louie's life and restored him almost to where he was before his crisis, have become like a family to us. They have all stopped by our room the last several days to tell Louie how great he looks and to tell him what a miracle he is and to give him hugs. All day Wednesday I cried at the drop of a hat. Everything anyone said to me brought on the tears.

Louie, too, experienced a lot of emotion that day. In the afternoon he had a slight panic attack as his mind reviewed all that had happened and all the expectations that accompanied his homecoming.

You will recall that I asked for prayer for Louie's "diabetes." Guess what! Today the nutritionist said that Louie has not had any insulin in the last three days. She recommended that he just come home and eat normally and check his sugar occasionally because his numbers are great right now! Yay! We will check with his family doctor in a few days, but I believe the diabetes is a thing of the past. Well, at least I know how to check someone's sugar now (have my own glucometer) and also know how to give an insulin shot. Hope I never have to do either!

We have promised the staff at LifeCare that we will go back for a visit as soon as Louie can walk without assistance. Today after a lot of tearful farewells and good wishes from the LifeCare staff, we left around 12:15 and arrived home about 1:15. Louie came home by ambulance so that we could have assistance getting him into the house safely. I really wanted to drive him, but we decided this might be the best plan.

We are now at home, and Louie is doing well using a walker to get around and is resting in his big recliner, which his nephew Carl very kindly heightened by adding a 6-inch base to the bottom of the chair. This makes it easier for Louie to get out of the chair. It's thoughtful deeds like this that have touched our hearts.

Neither of us can believe we are really home to stay. Words cannot describe how wonderful it is to be home!

Words also fail to describe the joy and gratitude we feel for the miracle God has given us. Louie and I continue to be blessed by people who have crossed our path during this trial and by the outpouring of love we have experienced from so many dear family members and friends. I could write a book just about all the wonderful encounters I have had with medical staff and family members of patients at both hospitals. God has truly been at work in both our lives, and we will never be the same again! It just amazes us how much joy we feel as we reflect on all that has happened.

Thank you for your many prayers. Please continue to pray for my cousin Jesse as he goes through his further treatments for pancreatic cancer. Also, I had a phone call from my son Eric this afternoon requesting prayer for a friend's dad. The dad's name is Tom, and he lives in Brownsville, TX. He has prostate cancer and apparently a multitude of other medical problems. Eric said he had shared with his friend Andrea how awesome the prayers of his mom's prayer circle are and that he would ask that this group pray for Tom I know you will add Tom to your prayers.

I'm attaching a picture Dana made of Louie with her mobile phone this afternoon. You may be able to tell that Louie has lost quite a bit of weight *[53 pounds]* during this ordeal, but he considers that one of the few perks of his long hospitalization!

People have asked if I ever was afraid along this journey. Of course I had some anxious moments. Those times when Louie was most critical were the most obvious ones. I felt fear rise up on a few other occasions as well. I remember when the first hospital statement arrived from Pitt Memorial just a few days after we had left there. That first statement, which did not include any doctors' fees, was enormous. We had been there six weeks, and I had no idea how long we would be at LifeCare. We were also expecting to have to go back to Pitt Memorial for rehab. The first thing that crossed my mind was, "Are Medicare and our other insurance policy going to cover these bills?"

We had never had such huge medical bills before, and I had no idea whether insurance would cover everything. I did feel great concern for a while regarding that first statement, realizing that there would be more to come for even larger amounts. However, after a short time of mulling it in my mind, I realized that just as I had given Louie to God's care, I had to give Him any financial concerns I had. I simply let it go and in faith trusted God to meet all our needs.

Later while we were at LifeCare, I remember becoming concerned as we neared the end of the number of days Medicare would pay for hospital care. Once again I had to entrust my concerns to God to handle, and He did!

Day after day, problem after problem, God was there to meet every need and to bring peace in the midst of the storm!

PART 3

THE JOURNEY CONTINUES

Chapter 15

God's Grace Is Sufficient

And He said to me, "My grace is sufficient for you, for My strength is made perfect in weakness. . ."
(2 Corinthians 12:9)

Once we were home, I was no longer sitting and waiting. My time for the next few weeks was spent taking care of Louie. At the hospital there had been many caregivers, and now I was the only one.

The first two days we were home, Louie chose to sleep in his recliner. It was so much easier for him to get out of his big chair with a little help from me than to get in and out of bed. I slept on the sofa in the den with him those first nights so that I could hear him if he needed me during the night.

My days were occupied with administering medicines, helping him with his bath, preparing his meals, changing the dressing on the stoma [opening] where his trach had been, helping him to the bathroom, etc.—all the things caregivers routinely do.

By the third night, Louie was ready to try sleeping in our king-sized bed. The only problem was that we had to switch sides so that he could get his walker close enough to his side of the bed. Because we are such creatures of habit, he did not sleep very well since he was on the wrong side of the bed. We tried this plan for several nights, and I finally suggested he try the queen-sized bed in another bedroom. Because he is so tall, he doesn't fit well in a regular bed, but the queen-sized bed worked quite well.

Then I was concerned that if he needed me, I might not hear him call from across the hall. His voice was still a little weak, and I was sleeping so soundly that I was afraid he would not wake me. So I came up with a plan for him to get my attention. I placed his cell phone beside his bed and had his phone programmed for speed dial to the house phone. If he needed me, all he had to do was pick up the phone and press 3. The house phone was right beside my bed, so I knew I would hear it. As funny as it seemed to be calling someone on the phone from across the hall, it made me feel better knowing he could wake me. The plan worked. I think he only needed to call me once using the phone when he needed help to get to the bathroom.

In the beginning Louie needed help getting out of the chair, getting on and off the potty seat, getting a bath, and getting in and out of bed. However, as the days passed, he improved each day. It was exciting to watch his progress. The first time he was able to get out of his chair or roll over in bed or get out of bed alone or take a shower—all were milestones.

The second week we were home we started having visits from our home health care agency. There were five people who were supposed to be helping us at home: a nurse, an aide, a physical therapist, an occupational therapist, and a speech therapist. The first time the aide came to assist Louie with his bath was in the after-noon. We quickly decided that we would not need an aide. Louie preferred his bath as soon as he got up, which was between 5 and 6 in the morning. Besides that, we often had visitors in the afternoon, and afternoon baths would just not be convenient. Personally, I had already decided that I would rather do it myself anyway. We told the aide we did not really need her services.

The nurse came to check on his vital signs, his stoma dressing, a pressure sore that had developed from his sitting all day, etc. After just a few visits, we felt we could handle his needs and didn't really need any outside nursing care.

The speech therapist came once and quickly determined that he was doing so well that her services also were not needed.

What we really needed at this point was the assistance of the physical and occupational therapists. This was something I could not do. They each came once a week for several weeks and worked with Louie to help him strengthen his muscles and learn to do things for himself. In the beginning Louie walked through the house with his walker. Eventually, his therapist had him going up and down the steps and walking outside.

It was exciting to see Louie daily becoming more independent. Each day we found more things to be thankful for. Always at the top of the list was God's mercy and the love of our family and friends. Friends continued to help with the lawn care and garden. Friends visited and brought us meals and baked goodies. Friends called and sent messages and cards of encouragement. Friends continued to pray for us.

There were many other milestones along the way. The first time we were able to go to church and Sunday School, I remember thinking as we entered church that morning, "My goodness, for the first time I feel that our lives have returned to normal!"

When we had been home about two weeks, I wrote to our dear friends at LifeCare to let them know of Louie's progress and to thank them for all they had done to help him recover. Here is the letter I sent and asked that it to be shared with all those whose lives had touched ours:

July 8, 2008

Dear LifeCare Family,

Louie and I have been home nearly two weeks now, and I wanted to let all of you know that he is doing very well. He continues to regain his strength and is walking better each day. He's now able to get up from his chair or the bed, get into bed alone, use the bathroom, and give himself a bath with very little help from me. We are very thankful for the progress he has made and is continuing to make.

We both would like to thank each of you for your contribution to Louie's recovery. Without the excellent treatment provided by Dr. Boseman, Dr. Cooper, John Apps, all the nurses and CNAs, the respiratory therapists, occupational therapists, physical therapists, speech therapists, the pharmacists, nutritionists, and others on the team, we know that his recovery would not have been so successful. Our hearts are full of love and gratitude to each one of who used your skills so effectively and gave us your love and attention as well. You became our family during our long stay at LifeCare, and we will always remember your commitment and many kindnesses.

I mentioned once at a rounds meeting to those present how I felt about our caregivers. Some of you may have missed what I said, so I want to share it with all of you. I hope that none of you ever finds yourself in the health crisis Louie was in. However, it is also my prayer that should that ever happen, you will be given the same loving care and attention that you have given to Louie.

We will both be spokespersons promoting LifeCare. You have truly blessed our lives. Your wonderful care and God's infinite grace and mercy have brought about a miracle! We are truly grateful to each of you.

In a few weeks when Louie is able to walk without the use of his walker, we plan to visit LifeCare for you to see all the progress he has made. While we are very excited to be home, we miss each of you and look forward to our visit.

We both pray God's richest blessings on each of you and LifeCare Hospital! I hope that this message will be shared with every single person who ministered to us while we were there. Also, please feel free to share this message with anyone who wants to know what a wonderful facility LifeCare is!

In Christ's love,

Carolyn and Louie Tyndall

On the 6-week anniversary of our homecoming, we were able to drive to Rocky Mount to visit Louie's caregivers at LifeCare in person. This is something we had been thinking about for weeks and had just been waiting until he felt comfortable walking in on his own with just the use of a cane.

It was a wonderful visit. Some of the nurses and even his pulmonary doctor had never seen Louie standing up. They marveled at how tall he is. It was like "going home" to see the dear friends we had made at the hospital. There were lots of smiles and hugs and tears at the reunion. I believe they were also truly blessed as they saw how all their wonderful care had paid off for Louie. Since we didn't get to see every single caregiver, we asked that those we visited share with the others how well Louie was doing.

Today Louie is continuing to improve. He still has a long way to go before he is as strong as before, but we see progress every day. This week he cut the grass using his riding lawnmower for the first time. He said it was the most fun he has ever had cutting the grass.

It has been a long journey, one that isn't over yet. While Louie often says that it was a journey he would not wish on anyone, both he and I recognize that God, in His infinite wisdom and by His permissive will, allowed this crisis into our lives for a purpose. We both know that we will never be the same again.

It would be too hard to recount all the blessings we've experienced as a result of this testing time, and surely Louie would have to speak for himself on how it has impacted him. I know from things he's shared with me and with others that his priorities in life have definitely changed. I believe he feels closer to his brother Robert than ever before as he saw Robert's concern for him while he was so sick. I believe his faith has grown immeasurably. His heart is full of gratitude as he recognizes that God has performed a miracle to save his life and restore him to health. I know he has a deeper appreciation and love for our friends who stood by us so faithfully.

I know that my relationship with Louie has changed as a result of this difficult time. We've grown closer than we have been in years. As a matter of fact, one of my most treasured gifts is what Louie gave me recently. I had been out to lunch with my friend, Mac Swanson, for the first such outing without Louie since we had returned home from the hospital. Louie had gone to lunch at the same time with my friend's husband, Glenn. When I returned home, Louie was already back from his lunch, and there was a gift bag in my chair. Inside was a beautiful little necklace with a sprinkling of tiny diamonds and a belated birthday card. While I loved the gift and the card, the real treasure was the note he had written and placed inside the card. It said

August 12, 2008

Dear Carolyn,

There are no words in the English language or any other language to say what is in my heart, but I will do the best I can.

Though I have no memory of much of my illness, I know from others that you dedicated your every moment to my getting well. And from the time I do remember, you were there for whatever I needed. I never heard one complaint or criticism. You encouraged me when I was not sure about the end results and reminded me of how far I had come. I was ready to meet God, and I think that gave me a great peace.

I can never repay you in any way for your dedication, your love and compassion, and your faith. As Dana says, you were Superwoman! I was able to come home and have no worries for you had taken care of every responsibility though I know not how you found time.

It has been quite obvious that your keeping people advised has touched many lives. My recovery is truly a miracle granted by the grace of God through many people.

I hope this little gift will remind you of my love for you and my appreciation for all that you have done and are doing. I would not have made it without you. You make me very proud to say you are my wife and the best nurse in the world!

All my love,

Louie

I certainly never felt I did anything beyond the call of duty while caring for Louie and definitely not anything that was not a labor of love, but I was very touched by his note.

As Louie said in his note, he doesn't remember much about his travail. As a matter of fact, he doesn't remember anything that happened while we were at Pitt Memorial, not even the first three days there while he was awaiting surgery. He doesn't remember being transported to LifeCare nor the first several weeks he was there in ICU. I've told him several times that this is another real blessing of God. Apparently, those countless times of sedation erased those memories, and for that I'm truly grateful. After we had been home a few weeks, Louie read a printed copy of all the e-mails I had sent regarding his hospital stay. I had only shared information with him in the hospital as I felt he was strong enough to cope with it. He learned most of the details of what had happened to him by reading those e-mail accounts of his progress once we were home.

His family doctor had requested a copy of all my e-mails to read my account of all the events that occurred while Louie was hospitalized. Both she and many of our friends suggested I write a book. This book is an outgrowth of those messages and the suggestions of many friends.

As we've traveled through this time of suffering, we've both grown more compassionate toward those who are experiencing illness and those taking care of sick loved ones.

There is a renewed appreciation for each day of life God has given us. For me, I feel even more urgency to live my life for Christ as I have recognized how fragile life really is.

We appreciate the faithfulness of our friends more than ever, and we recognize as never before the power of prayer. We are able to see the good things God has brought about in our lives and the lives of others as a result of this journey.

Life itself is definitely a journey, and we should not be waiting until we reach some imaginary place in life to begin to live and to serve the Lord. People often use the excuses, "When I am old enough," "When I get the job of my dreams," "When I meet the right man (or woman)," "When I have more money," "When I feel better," "When I don't have any problems," "When I know more scripture," "When I am good enough," "When I retire," "When my children are grown," and countless other procrastinating "whens" to delay living life to the fullest. God is not preparing us to live for Him and to serve Him *when* He gets us prepared. The journey is IT! Even a journey through a crisis is part of God's plan for our lives in order to grow us up in Himself and for us to be used to His glory!

I don't wish for you, dear reader, or anyone else to travel our particular journey; but if you are alive, and you have to be to read these words, you are going to experience some trials too. Perhaps yours will be very different from those we experienced, but they will be testing times. My prayer for each reader is that you will trust God throughout your own personal journey. He, and only He, is the real Rock you will need to lean on. He will be your Peace in the middle of life's storms. Remember to look for His blessings along the way.

Our story is not over. God blessed us and brought us safely through this trial. Neither of us knows how much longer God will give us here on this earth or what other tests we will have to endure. While life is just as precious, probably even more so, as it was in our younger years, there is no promise for tomorrow. Things may not turn out this well the next time. However, our faith and peace do not rest on the outcome of our tests but rather on the strength God gives us along the way. As long as we continue to walk in God's will, He will be our mainstay, and we will trust Him. It is, after all, the journey that counts!

THE BEGINNING
(of the next journey!)

Printed in the United States
221720BV00001B/85/P